W9-BVU-611

WINNING THE FIGHT

WITH COURAGE

FOR A

AND CLOTH

WOMAN'S RIGHT TO VOTE

ANN BAUSUM

NATIONAL GEOGRAPHIC

WASHINGTON, D.C.

FOR THE PRESENT WITH DAN

FOR THE PAST
AND ALL THE WOMEN WHO FOUGHT SO LONG FOR SUFFRAGE

FOR THE FUTURE
AND THE YOUNG PEOPLE WHO WILL VOTE TOMORROW

AB

Text copyright © 2004 Ann Bausum

Published by the National Geographic Society.
All rights reserved. Reproduction of the whole or any part of the contents without written permission
from the National Geographic Society is strictly prohibited.

Library of Congress Cataloging-in-Publication Data
Bausum, Ann.
With courage and cloth : winning the fight for a woman's right to vote / by Ann Bausum.
p. cm.
Includes bibliographical references.
Trade Edition ISBN 0-7922-7647-7
Library Edition ISBN 0-7922-6996-9
1. Women—Suffrage—United States—History. I. Title.
JK1896.B38 2004
324.6'23'0973—dc22
2004001191

Printed in China

Book design by Bea Jackson
Production design by Ruth Thompson, Thunder Hill Graphics
Text is set in Mrs. Eaves, designed by Zuzana Licko, Emigre.
Display font is Ashley Inline and sans serif text throughout is Radiant by Font Company.

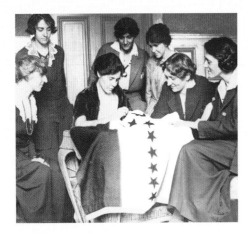

In 1919 Alice Paul (seated, center) began to sew what was probably the last banner from the fight for a woman's right to vote. She started with her National Woman's Party signature colors—purple, white, and golden yellow. Then, each time a state ratified the proposed 19th Amendment to the U.S. Constitution, Paul sewed another gold star onto her banner.

The design motif of this book pays tribute to this banner. The photographs have been colorized in duotone combinations of purple and golden yellow, and these colors appear throughout the book. In an echo of Paul's sewing ceremony, each chapter opener adds another star to the banner design at the top of the page.

Chapter opener quotes are taken from the chapter text and are attributed in the source notes beginning on page 102.

TABLE OF CONTENTS

ONCE ALICE PAUL AND I stood head to head and eye to eye. I was 13 years old; she was 86. We must have looked one another over carefully, because it's her strong gaze, more than anything else, that I've remembered. My father, who introduced us, explained at the time how this wizened old woman had fought years earlier for my right to vote. I didn't doubt it. Plenty of flame remained in her eyes.

What surprised me then was the discovery that women had had to fight at all in order to vote. After all, my mother went to the polls alongside my father. Hadn't it always been that way? Apparently not.

My childhood history books made no mention of Alice Paul and a fight for women's voting rights. Those books were filled with stories about generals and armies, wars and victories. I knew all about Washington and Lee, Marshall and Eisenhower. History seemed to be a progression of stories about men and wars and conquest. Except for a few scattered figures, women had apparently stayed home while history happened. It was not until I set aside my childhood books and shook the hand of Alice Paul that a fuller view of U.S. history began to emerge.

In August 1920 Alice Paul (left) sewed the final star on her ratification banner and toasted passage of the 19th Amendment to the Constitution. The occasion marked the official end of the fight for a woman's right to vote in the U.S.

Near the end of her life—some 50 years after passage of the 19th Amendment—Alice Paul posed with the Great Demand Banner from the fight for women's voting rights.

That's a shame, because the history of how American women fought for and won their right to vote is one of the great stories about the growth of our nation. It is a tale of courage and adventure, challenge and skill, patience and hope. Countless women—and a few men, too—fought campaigns not unlike those waged by an army at war. Although the fight was less bloody, it lasted much longer than any U.S. conflict. Indeed, almost from the earliest days of colonization, and certainly by the time of Abigail Adams, women had begun calling for equality with men. The closely fought battle for women's voting rights spanned the 72 years from 1848 to 1920. Fighters for this cause, instead of taking up guns and swords, armed themselves with courage and cloth.

8

Cloth was a fitting choice. It was a substance all women knew intimately, having woven, sewn, cleaned, and mended it for generations. It was readily available, and everyone knew how to use it. Women turned it into sashes, made it into signs, and sewed it into flags. Just choosing to wear clothing of a certain color—the signature choice was white—put a woman into uniform for the fight.

Those women who took up the cause during the 19th century, such as Susan B. Anthony, Elizabeth Cady Stanton, and Lucy Stone, would not live to see it end. The generation that finished the task—including Alice Paul—had not been born when the work began. Some women devoted their fortunes to the cause, others gave their lives. Some denied themselves the comforts of marriage and family in order to dedicate all their energy to the fight. Others broke ties with loved ones so they could continue their work. Even when the goal was beyond the grasp of their own lifetimes, they fought on.

> ★
>
> *"We are bearing on the American tradition, living up to the American spirit."*
>
> –ALICE PAUL
> November 27, 1917

They fought on so that girls of 13 (and boys, too) would grow up in a world where women may, of course, vote with ease.

Perhaps because of my meeting with Alice Paul, I've focused in this book on the years of history she helped shape. This period, from 1913 to 1920, is often overlooked or simplified in other histories about women's voting rights. In order to view the end of the story in context, however, I've included a summary of what came before it. In addition, readers will find a comprehensive chronology of the campaign for women's voting rights in the reference section at the end of the book. Accompanying profiles highlight significant leaders in the fight.

May these women take their places equally with their male counterparts in the chronicles of U.S. history.

★

CHAPTER ONE

1913

PARADE

"We demand an amendment. . ."

IN 1913 ALICE PAUL HELPED PLAN a parade. It wasn't the nation's first demonstration in support of votes for women, and it wasn't the last one. This parade became a turning point, though, in the 72-year struggle for the right of women to vote in the United States.

Alice Paul organized the parade just as a general might plan for battle. Timing was crucial. The event was set for Monday, March 3, the day before the Inauguration of the nation's 28th President, Woodrow Wilson. Alice Paul and her collaborators knew that plenty of people, including the media, would be on hand already for that occasion and would see and report about their event. Location was critical, too. They insisted that the parade follow the same prestigious route reserved for the Inaugural procession.

A small army of volunteers helped design floats, recruit bands, and enlist marchers for the event. Organizers wanted so many women to gather from so many places and with such a varied set of credentials that their presence would be overwhelming. Surely no one—not news reporters, not business leaders, not lawmakers, not the man on the street, not even the

Alice Paul and associates planned two companion events to support their voting rights parade. A group of women and children staged a pageant on the steps of the U.S. Treasury Building about democracy as the parade began. In one scene, the actress Hedwig Reicher (in the flag-striped cape) portrayed the figure of "Columbia." After the pageant and parade, women gathered in Constitution Hall for the day's final event, a rally for the cause.

Inez Milholland (above, on horse) played the role of herald, or messenger, during the 1913 parade in Washington, D.C., for women's voting rights. She rode at the head of the procession carrying a golden banner. The text, "Forward out of darkness, forward into light," became a motto for Alice Paul and fellow activists.

newly elected President of the United States—would miss the point. Women, whatever their differences, were committed to one common goal: They wanted the right to vote.

As many as 8,000 women converged on Washington, D.C., to take part in the march. Many participants arrived by car or other means of modern transportation. Some made symbolic treks on foot from as far away as New York State. They were welcomed on March 3 by crisp weather, a cloudless sky, and an estimated 500,000 spectators.

Inez Milholland, a beautiful young attorney, set forth past the U.S. Capitol building at the head of the afternoon procession. She was dressed all in white, riding an all-white horse, and she looked like a modern-day Joan of Arc. "We demand an amendment to the Constitution of the United States enfranchising the women of the country," read the Great Demand Banner proceeding after her.

Six "divisions" of women followed, each one representing a theme about women's rights. Some participants rode on floats, others were on horseback, most walked. The parade featured groups of women doctors, women nurses, women lawyers, women business leaders, women artists, and women educators. Women gathered to represent their clubs, states, religious groups, the Red Cross, the PTA, and political parties. Wives and daughters of congressmen (there were no congresswomen yet) joined the parade. African Americans were encouraged to march in a segregated group near the end of the lineup. At least one—Ida B. Wells-Barnett from Chicago— insisted on marching alongside her white suffrage friends from Illinois.

Colorful splashes of cloth dotted the scene. Street vendors had sold thousands of yellow Votes for Women pennants. Bunting, or festive hangings, of the same color—a traditional hue for the women's campaign—had been added alongside the Inaugural decorations of red, white, and blue. Countless marchers wore yellow badges or sashes on their costumes that demanded Votes for Women. Many were clothed in the all-white attire that signified support for their cause.

Numerous cloth banners identified the various groups of marchers. Other banners, bearing instructive messages, hung from floats or hand-held poles. Many of these standards featured a new trio of colors for the movement: purple for justice, white for purity of purpose, and gold for courage.

Milholland, proceeding on her white steed, turned onto Pennsylvania Avenue. The White House and the end of her march lay ahead. The parade stretched out fully formed behind. It ranged from an opening section about the voting rights of women in other countries to a closing division of representatives from the United States—including groups of supportive men. Alice Paul, recipient of three academic degrees, marched midway in the procession with a sizeable delegation of college graduates. She must have felt proud.

With the help of others, Paul had recruited literally thousands of women, armed them with cloth banners, and organized them to march in regiment-style groups. The diversity, unity, and determination of these

What started as an orderly procession down a wide boulevard became a fight through a narrowing funnel as the U.S. Capitol faded into the distance and the parade inched toward the White House. A few marchers dropped from the ranks to avoid continued harassment. Others persisted, at times in tears. Mothers encouraged their marching children to persevere and sheltered them as best they could from the menacing crowd.

"troops" was unmistakable. A conquering army could not have looked more courageous or full of purpose.

There was only one problem: The crowd didn't like what it saw. Perhaps the onlookers, who were mostly men, were intimidated by the sight of so many women organized to seek power. Many who watched were out-of-towners already in a partying mood because of the upcoming Inauguration. Perhaps these visitors had expected to be amused by the spectacle of women on parade. What they saw instead—an overwhelming force of feminine vitality—was no laughing matter.

Spectators, particularly the white men, began to harass the marchers. They broke past restraining ropes, tailed the procession, pushed, shouted insults and obscenities, and pinched and spat at the passing women. They threatened marchers, tore off their badges, touched the exposed skin of costumed women on floats, and attempted to climb aboard the passing wagons. The pace of the parade slowed as the crowd pressed closer, narrowing the women's path from the width of a multilane street to the span of a single car. Finally even that minimal space evaporated.

Police officers (who were all male) did little to restrain the crowd or protect the marchers. Women reported later that most policemen had stood idly by, smiling and laughing at the scene. Perhaps they felt as unsympathetic to the cause as did the spectators. "There would be nothing like this if you women would all stay at home," suggested one officer. One marcher complained that the police "would have taken better care of a drove of pigs." Another observed: "There seemed to be a tacit agreement to make our efforts a failure."

As the parade deteriorated into a near riot, a few sympathetic men stepped forward to help. A regiment of National Guard troops—on hand for the Inaugural parade of the next day—pushed back the crowd at one intersection. A group of male college students linked arms at another to clear a path for marchers cut off from the main procession. Boy Scouts used their walking staffs to restrain spectators elsewhere. Federal cavalry troops—placed on alert by the secretary of war at Paul's urging—were called upon to help restore order. Even so, a projected two-hour march dragged on until nearly nightfall.

Newspaper coverage of the event exceeded even Paul's expectations. (Radio and television news broadcasts had yet to be invented.) There were plenty of reports about the parade itself.

★

"Yesterday the government, which is supposed to exist for the good of all, left women while passing in peaceful procession . . .at the mercy of a howling mob."

–HARRIOT STANTON BLATCH
March 4, 1913
telegram sent to President Woodrow Wilson as he started his Inaugural parade

But there were news stories, too, about the subsequent investigation by the U.S. Senate into the lack of police protection for marchers. Reporters wrote about the eventual dismissal of the capital's police chief, as well. The right of women to vote was transformed overnight from the special interest of a few persistent activists into a national topic of discussion.

Parades might come and go, but the cause of votes for women would not fall far from public view again. There were literally thousands of women—including Alice Paul—who would see to that.

★ ★

CHAPTER TWO

1 8 4 8 - 1 9 0 6

RIGHTS

"To do and dare anything"

WHEN FIVE WIVES AND MOTHERS organized a meeting about the rights of women in 1848, they didn't know they would make history. They didn't even know if anyone would show up. After their meeting ended—with a larger turnout and greater success than expected—still no one saw the events at Seneca Falls, New York, as the beginning of a movement. It wasn't until decades later that people looking back began to see how, more than anywhere else, the fight for women's rights—especially the right to vote—began at Seneca Falls.

The meeting at Seneca Falls would never have happened without one of its newest residents: Elizabeth Cady Stanton. Stanton—a capable wife and the mother of three young boys—hated the drudgery of ceaseless housework in this sleepy country town. She yearned for the comforts of the well-staffed home in the heart of Boston where she had lived just 13 months before.

So, when Stanton sat down for tea with four friends on July 13, 1848, she did what any frustrated woman might do. She complained. Stanton complained not only about her own situation, but about how women

Many "Antis"—people opposed to granting women access to the polls—believed the whole American way of life would collapse if women voted. Family dynamics would be turned upside down. (Might husbands have to take over doing the laundry?!) Antis feared that husbands and wives would argue over politics. One U.S. senator predicted that independent women would "make every home a hell on earth." Satirists gave vision to these worst-case scenarios (including this staged photo of a washerman and his wife) throughout the campaign for a woman's right to vote.

everywhere suffered because they were not treated equally by men. Her feelings were so intense that, she later recalled, "I stirred myself, as well as the rest of the party, to do and dare anything."

Stanton and her companions decided to hold a "convention," or meeting, to "discuss the social, civil and religious condition and rights of Woman." Then they drafted "A Declaration of Rights and Sentiments" to summarize their concerns. "When in the course of human events," began their text, which they modeled after the Declaration of Independence. They added "and women" to the famous phrase that "all men are created equal."

Their document included 12 ways to foster equality for women in such areas as education, law, labor, morality, and religion. The ninth one called for women to vote. It read: "Resolved, that it is the duty of the women of this country to secure to themselves their sacred right to the elective franchise."

Lucretia Mott, one of the organizers, argued that a resolution about a woman's right to vote was too bold and should be dropped lest it "make us [look] ridiculous." Elizabeth Cady Stanton persuaded her that the text must remain: How could women change biased laws if they could not vote? Stanton's husband, Henry, was so shocked by the thought of women voting that he left town during the meeting to avoid all association with the idea.

Elizabeth Cady Stanton's call for voting rights aroused the most debate after the convention opened on July 19, 1848. Many participants felt this demand was too bold and would hurt the credibility of other points. Stanton argued in support of it, as did audience member Frederick Douglass, the prominent former slave. (No one recorded whether African-American women attended the convention, too.)

★

"Oh! How I do repent me of the male faces I have washed, the mittens I have knit, the pants mended, the cut fingers and broken toes I have bound up. . . ."

–ELIZABETH CADY STANTON
March 21, 1871
writing to Martha Coffin Wright,
a Seneca Falls organizer and
sister of Lucretia Mott

Stanton's resolution for women's voting rights passed by a slim majority. All others passed unanimously during meetings that filled 18 hours over the span of two days. A third of the 300 participants—68 women and 32 men—signed the declaration, including three of the five organizers' husbands.

Typical of comments made after the convention were the ones of a local reporter who noted that the proposals, if adopted, "would set the world by the ears." Frederick Douglass noted sympathetically that "a discussion of the rights of animals would be regarded with more complacency by many . . . than would a discussion of the rights of women."

Seneca Falls was the equivalent of the Boston Tea Party or the battle of Lexington and Concord in what became an extended campaign for women's voting rights. Just as those events had done during the Revolutionary War, Seneca Falls got people's attention.

Then the question became "What do we do next?" Men weren't going to just give women what they wanted. A few men supported the idea of equality, but most were comfortable with the world as it was. They held the power and saw no reason to share it, especially by letting women vote.

Sometimes voting is called "suffrage," a word that comes from the Latin *suffragium,* meaning "approval" and "the right to vote." Someone who works to gain voting rights is often called a suffragist. Sometimes women who sought suffrage were called suffragettes; often this term was used with a tone of disapproval. Most women referred to themselves as suffragists, not suffragettes, and that is what they're called today.

"Franchise" is another word used to describe voting. It evolved from an Old French word that meant "freedom." People with voting rights are enfranchised. Those without them are disenfranchised, or simply

★

"The ladies always have the best place and choicest tidbit at the table. They have the best seat in the cars. . . . If there is any inequity or oppression in the case, the gentlemen are the sufferers."

–SAMUEL A. FOOTE
March 1856
commenting as a New York State legislator about a petition from 6,000 women seeking increased rights

The fight for woman suffrage extended through multiple generations of more than one family. Elizabeth Cady Stanton and her daughter Harriot (top) worked for the cause for much of their adult lives. Even Stanton's granddaughter, Nora, grew old enough to take up the fight. During many of the same years, suffrage pioneer Lucy Stone collaborated with her daughter, Alice (bottom), at gaining voting rights for women.

disfranchised. In suffrage campaigns people may speak of seeking the franchise. They mean they want the right to vote.

The first women suffragists, including Elizabeth Cady Stanton and Lucretia Mott, were champions for another cause, too: abolishing slavery. They saw parallels between the oppression of women and the oppression of slaves. If white men could be persuaded to free African-American slaves, surely they would see the justice in granting more rights to women, too.

Other women who supported both causes were Lucy Stone and Susan B. Anthony. Mott, who was 55 at the Seneca Falls convention, was the oldest of the group. Stanton, 32, was next. Stone, 29, and Anthony, 28, (both not at this first meeting) were younger still.

These pioneers and countless others— including some men who joined them—were, with rare exception, white. They petitioned state legislatures to change laws unfair to women, made speeches, wrote letters, published news stories, and argued for their beliefs.

Although Sojourner Truth is best known for her efforts to end slavery, she should be remembered as the first woman suffragist of color, as well. She spoke eloquently about the oppression of women in the years after Seneca Falls. "Ain't I a woman?" she insisted when men suggested that women were not the equals of men. "I have ploughed, and planted, and gathered into barns, and no man could head me!" stated Truth at an 1851 woman's rights convention in Akron, Ohio. "And ain't I a woman? I could work as much and eat as much as a man— when I could get it—and bear the lash as well! And ain't I a woman?"

Meetings like these took place exclusively in the North. With slavery as a guiding principle in the South, women there could barely imagine change, much less expect to voice such thoughts publicly.

After the Civil War broke out in 1861, northern women set aside the fight for their own rights and supported the war effort. They became nurses, sewed war supplies, and took over jobs left behind by soldiers. Many expected that, when the war ended, the former slaves would gain the right to vote along with their freedom. Surely the loyal wartime service of women would earn them a share in this expansion of rights. It did not. When the Civil War ended on April 9, 1865, male lawmakers and abolitionists worked to correct the mistakes of slavery, but women's issues were pushed aside to be dealt with later.

Former slaves gained new rights thanks to revisions to the U.S. Constitution. This document established the federal government in 1788. In order for it to be amended, or changed, two-thirds of the members of Congress must agree to the proposal. Then three-fourths of the state legislatures must ratify, or approve, it. (The Constitution has been amended 27 times.)

The 13th Amendment outlawed slavery in 1865. Two related amendments followed soon after, but neither granted women the right to vote. In fact, they made the prospect more doubtful. The 14th Amendment became law in 1868. Among other things, it promised all adult *male* citizens over the age of 21 the right to vote. Until then the Constitution had never mentioned gender. The 15th Amendment followed in 1870. It strengthened the right of citizens to vote regardless of "race, color, or previous condition of servitude." The text made no mention of rights based on gender.

Disagreements developed among women suffragists about these oversights, and old allies divided into two camps. Stanton and Anthony, who had become fast friends, condemned the newest amendments. They organized their resistance into the National Woman Suffrage Association (called NWSA or the "National") in May 1869. Before the year was out,

Lucy Stone had founded the American Woman Suffrage Association (known as AWSA or the "American") for her followers. Mott, in her late 70s by then, tried to maintain peace between the two factions, but with little success.

The National organization of Stanton and Anthony was decidedly more radical and militant than Stone's group. Men could not join. The organization worked to defeat passage of the 15th Amendment. Members—almost all of whom were white—insisted that educated women deserved suffrage ahead of illiterate former slaves. Stanton and Anthony founded a weekly newspaper, *The Revolution,* with the motto "Men, their rights and nothing more; women their rights and nothing less!"

Lucy Stone remained sympathetic to former slaves and supported the new amendments. "I will be thankful in my soul if *any* body can get out of the terrible pit" of being disenfranchised, she claimed. She established the *Woman's Journal* to spread the American's more moderate message. Members of this much larger organization (who were female and male, black and white) organized themselves into independent state chapters.

> ★
>
> *"We ask that all the civil and political rights that belong to citizens of the United States be guaranteed to us and our daughters forever."*
>
> –SUSAN B. ANTHONY
> July 4, 1876
> from the
> "Declaration of Rights for Women,"
> presented on the nation's centennial

Both groups soon agreed on one thing: The only way to gain votes for women was with new laws. Beyond that point, however, the thinking diverged. Stanton and Anthony wanted another federal amendment to correct the omission of women from the 14th and 15th ones. Stone preferred to work for the right of women to vote in state elections. She thought legislators would support a federal amendment only after they saw women vote responsibly in the states.

Stanton and Anthony decided the state route would be too slow and labor-intensive; they concentrated their fight on the federal level. In 1878 they managed to have a woman suffrage amendment introduced for consideration by the U.S. Senate. Nine years passed before the measure came to a vote. Then it flopped. Only 16 senators (out of 76) supported it (including no one from the South). Thirty-four opposed it, and another 26 abstained from voting at all. The U.S. House of Representatives avoided all consideration of woman suffrage until well past the end of the century.

Meanwhile, Stone and her American suffragists organized literally hundreds of attempts to have those people who could vote—men—consider referenda that would expand the voting rights of women in state elections. (Referenda, plural for referendum, are specific votes held about the possible change of the law.) How might women hope to influence these male voters? Lucy Stone offered this advice for wives with unsupportive husbands: "When he says good morning, tell him you want to vote; when he asks what you are going to have for dinner, tell him you want to vote; and whatever he asks from the time you rise up in the morning until you lie down at night, tell him you want to vote."

Despite such persistence—and much broader efforts besides—only a handful of these referenda even made it onto a state ballot between 1870 and 1910. Of these only two passed: Colorado in 1893 and Idaho in 1896. Several United States territories offered women the right to vote during the 19th century. Two of them included woman suffrage in their constitutions when they earned statehood: Wyoming in 1890

Elizabeth Cady Stanton (right) and Susan B. Anthony worked as a team, "like two sticks of a drum. . .keeping up. . .the rub-a-dub of agitation." Stanton—who by 1859 was tied to home life with seven children—wrote speeches for the single Anthony to deliver. Stanton would sometimes ask Anthony to visit and help. "You must make the puddings and carry the baby while I ply the pen" to create a new speech.

and Utah in 1896. These western suffrage gains came as much because voting women were needed to support the existing white male power base as because of broad-minded generosity.

A few state and local governments granted women "partial suffrage" in local elections and on matters concerning education. Otherwise no more gains were made. Plenty of states, especially those east of the Mississippi, gave no consideration to the matter at all. (*See map page 34 for a view of the evolving regional support for woman suffrage.*)

New Jersey allowed women to vote equally with men until party politics led legislators to ban the practice in 1807. More than 80 years would pass before any state permitted women to vote again. (Four western territories did offer woman suffrage during this time.) In the years following the Civil War a handful of women—white and African-American—tried to vote and challenge these bans, but few were successful. By the century's end women could vote without restriction in only four sparsely populated western states. New voters headed to the polls in Colorado (above) starting in 1893.

The period from 1896 to 1910 (during which no states adopted woman suffrage) became known as the "doldrums" of the movement. The wind seemed to go out of the sails of the cause. No matter how hard suffragists argued in support of votes for women, they could not muster the momentum to overcome the antisuffragists, or "Antis," who opposed them.

Men everywhere seemed to fear the influence of women voters—from legislators to members of the clergy to business tycoons to liquor vendors to machine politicians to new immigrant voters. "I want to go [home], not to the embrace of some female ward politician, but to the earnest loving look and touch of a true woman," observed one U.S. senator. Plenty of women opposed suffrage, too. They wanted to avoid the unseemly business of politics; they preferred to use their influence behind the scenes. Antis believed that fathers and husbands represented the interests of women at the polls already. (Single adult women were just out of luck, apparently.)

Many Southerners—especially white men—opposed any extension of suffrage to women—particularly to black women. These men even worked to disenfranchise black males. By the turn of the century they had essentially done so through the use of biased literacy tests, civics quizzes, poll taxes, and downright intimidation. Non-Southerners, many of whom harbored their own racial prejudices, turned a "blind eye" to these discriminatory practices. After all, it was the states' responsibility to hold "free and fair" elections. Local leaders stretched their authority until it seemed to be their "states' right" to sidestep federal laws in favor of local practices.

Some people, including the growing number of African-American men and women who supported woman suffrage, genuinely wanted "universal" voting rights for all races and genders. However, some suffragists—both in the North and an emerging number of advocates in the South—sought to increase support for their cause by suggesting a more sinister logic: If women gained suffrage, white women could outvote the combined total of black men and women. By granting voting rights to women, therefore, white supremacy over blacks could grow even stronger. (This racist argument persisted off and on for the rest of the suffrage fight.)

Lucretia Mott died in 1880, still hoping her old allies Stanton, Anthony, and Stone would reunite. Ten years later, after extensive negotiations, they did. The National (NWSA) and American (AWSA) merged into the National American Woman Suffrage Association, or NAWSA, on February 18, 1890. This organization survived to the conclusion of the suffrage fight 30 years later.

Stone (now 72) and Stanton (74) assumed roles in the new alliance. But Anthony (70), took the lead. In the final years of her life, she strengthened the organization, extended its reach throughout the country, and recruited wealthy women to support the cause. Stone died in 1893, Stanton nine years after that, and Anthony in 1906. In her final speech, Anthony praised the persistence of suffragists: "With such women consecrating their lives . . . failure is impossible!"

TORTURING WOMEN IN PRISON

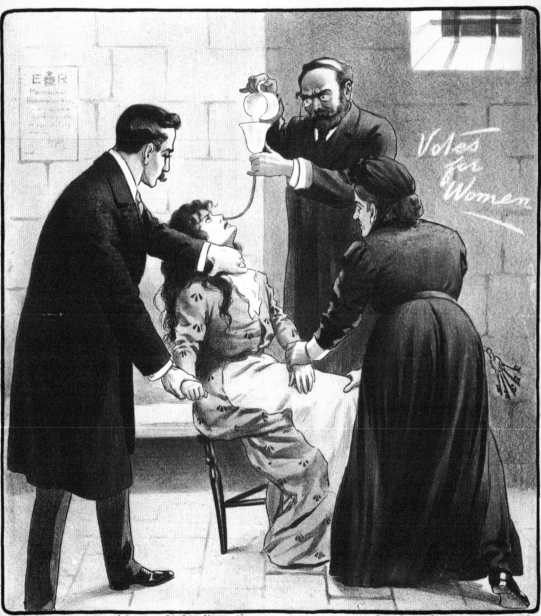

Votes for Women

PUBLISHED BY THE NATIONAL WOMEN'S SOCIAL AND POLITICAL UNION 4 CLEMENTS INN STRAND W.C. & PRINTED BY DAVID ALLEN & SONS LD 180 FLEET ST E.C.

VOTE AGAINST THE GOVERNMENT

CHAPTER THREE

★ ★ ★

1906 – 1916

MOMENTUM

"We have to take a new departure."

WHILE U.S. SUFFRAGISTS WERE STUCK in the doldrums at the turn of the century, their sisters across the Atlantic were sailing full speed ahead for the cause of woman suffrage. By 1906 some British women were using civil disobedience—deliberate disregard of custom and law—in an attempt to gain voting rights. Their actions became increasingly militant as demands went unmet. The radical women held demonstrations, shouted down government speakers, and threw stones through office windows. They set fires in mailboxes, cut telephone wires, vandalized train cars, and burned down buildings. The media scornfully called the women "suffragettes," a term they accepted with pride.

Police reacted to these protests with brutality, and many women were arrested and jailed. Prisoners protested their rough treatment by starting hunger strikes. Jailers retaliated with aggressive, even savage force-feedings of the women. In short order more than a thousand suffragettes had spent time in jail, and scores had been force-fed.

Harriot Stanton Blatch, the youngest daughter of Elizabeth Cady Stanton, was well acquainted with British activists. She had lived in Great

British suffragists sought attention for their cause in the opening years of the 20th century with a poster campaign. Notices called attention to such injustices as the force-feeding of jailed suffrage protesters. This one asks sympathetic male voters to defeat those officials who were responsible for the practice.

In 1913 Elizabeth Cady Stanton's granddaughter, Nora Blatch (center, left), promoted suffrage at open-air meetings during the "New York State horseback crusade." Her mother, Harriot Blatch, had helped popularize outdoor speeches. Harriot thought streets made an "ideal auditorium for those who are trying to push an unpopular cause." Speakers might mount steps, climb a statue, or stand on tables and chairs. Sometimes, instead of lecturing, women marched wearing signs with lines from a "voiceless speech."

Britain for two decades and collaborated with them there. When she moved home to the United States in 1896, she noted that, by comparison, "There did not seem to be a grain of political knowledge in the [U.S.] movement." Blatch changed that fact. She interested working women in voting rights, arranged speaking tours by British suffragettes, recruited wealthy supporters of the cause, and established an annual New York City suffrage parade. A young college graduate noted: "As for the suffrage movement, it is actually fashionable now." Perhaps "suffrage was a thing to fight for, suffer for, even to die for," suggested another after attending a suffragette lecture.

By this point a growing number of southern women wanted suffrage, either for themselves or as a way to assure white supremacy over African Americans. Some organized the Southern States Woman Suffrage Conference to promote suffrage as a states' right. They opposed a federal amendment. Others supported NAWSA. Most of them—and their northern sisters, too—supported suffrage for women of color when it advanced their hopes of votes for all women. Yet they might downplay universal suffrage when they thought it could hurt their own chances.

Black suffragists worked alongside whites when they were permitted to do so, sometimes insisting on this right as Ida B. Wells-Barnett did during the 1913 suffrage parade. At the same time they organized segregated clubs to raise support for the cause among other African Americans.

Blatch's work and the arrival of a new generation of activists helped end the U.S. suffrage doldrums. The logjam broke with a string of victories, starting with Washington State in 1910—the first such gain in 14 years. Women won suffrage in populous California a year later. The tally of states where women could vote grew to nine in 1912 with wins in Kansas, Arizona, and Oregon. By 1913 when Illinois lawmakers authorized women to vote in the state's presidential election, women could influence 84 of the 483 members of the electoral college. (These state representatives have the final say on who becomes President after Election Day ballots are counted.)

The newest suffragists were too young to have worked with Stanton, Anthony, and Stone. One of them was Alice Paul. In 1908 Paul, age 23, discovered the radical British suffrage scene. She became a suffragette while studying in London and was arrested at least seven times in Great Britain. Tough in spite of her frail frame, she survived jail on three occasions, participated in hunger strikes, and was force-fed.

In 1910 Paul met Lucy Burns—a robust Irish American with flaming red hair—at a London police station. (They had just been arrested.) The women protested together after their release until Paul returned to the United States later that year. Burns stayed. She invested three years in the British movement and made four visits to prison. When she returned to the United States in 1912, she renewed her collaboration with Paul.

★

"The right to become citizens of the state is the next and inevitable consequence of education and work outside the home. We have gone so far; we must go farther. We cannot go back."

–MARTHA CAREY THOMAS
1908
president of Bryn Mawr College
to the National College Women's
Equal Suffrage League

Young girls joined their mothers and other women in a march to the U.S. Capitol on May 9, 1914. They delivered a petition asking legislators to support voting rights for women.

In order to promote the cause of voting rights, women filled trains with teams of traveling activists, dropped leaflets from airplanes, and set up suffrage booths at carnivals, among other tactics. They posted their slogans on everything from billboards, to parade animals, to tugboats (above, within sight of New York City). Whatever the method, the message was the same: We want votes for women!

The two women complemented one another perfectly, not unlike the match between Stanton and Anthony. "They seemed in those early days to have one spirit and one brain," a mutual friend observed.

By the beginning of 1913 Paul and Burns, as members of NAWSA, were sent to work in Washington, D.C. They were expected to rekindle interest in a federal amendment for woman suffrage by helping the group's so-called Congressional Committee (women assigned to lobby, or persuade, lawmakers to support federal legislation). Their first effort was the massive suffrage parade on March 3 that preceded the Inauguration of Woodrow Wilson.

Paul—aided by Burns and a growing staff—kept the momentum going after the parade. They led delegations of suffragists to visit the President. They worked with others to collect suffrage petitions, raised thousands of dollars for the cause, and started a weekly newspaper, *The Suffragist.* They identified thousands of supporters nationwide and organized them into state chapters. The Congressional Committee's work quickly expanded from its original basement headquarters to ten rooms on two floors.

NAWSA leaders were startled by this rapid growth. The Congressional Committee had taken on a life of its own. Suddenly it seemed to be competing with its parent organization for members and financial support. Paul's forceful tactics were attracting criticism as too bold and "unwomanly," as well. NAWSA officials—aware of Paul's prior experience with the increasingly controversial suffragettes in Great Britain—worried about what she might do next.

Suffrage history repeated itself. In 1914 U.S. suffragists divided themselves once again into two camps. As before, the larger, more conservative group primarily sought suffrage through the states, while Paul's smaller, more radical organization focused on a federal amendment. Eventually her group became known as the National Woman's Party.

In 1914, probably due to increased pressure from Paul's organization, U.S. senators held their first vote on woman suffrage in 27 years. It was not a success. More than a third of the senators abstained from voting. Of those who did vote, only a one-vote majority (35 to 34) favored suffrage, nowhere near the required two-thirds majority of 64 votes. When the U.S. House of Representatives held its first-ever vote on woman suffrage ten months later, the measure was defeated. There were 174 in favor and 204 opposed, or almost 100 votes shy of the total needed. State suffrage fared little better. Of the 13 state referenda held on woman suffrage between 1914 and 1916, only two of them—in the sparsely populated western states of Montana and Nevada—gained approval.

> ★
>
> *"Women are not in rebellion against men. They are in rebellion against worn-out traditions."*
>
> –CARRIE CHAPMAN CATT
> June 1914

Women advocating for suffrage fought against increasingly well-organized opponents. By 1915 Antis had organized a National Association Opposed to Woman Suffrage with 200,000 members, and chapters in more than half of the states. Unsympathetic governors routinely refused to place referenda on statewide ballots. Many referenda were defeated by suspicious

Suffrage Conditions Prior to the 19th Amendment, August 1920

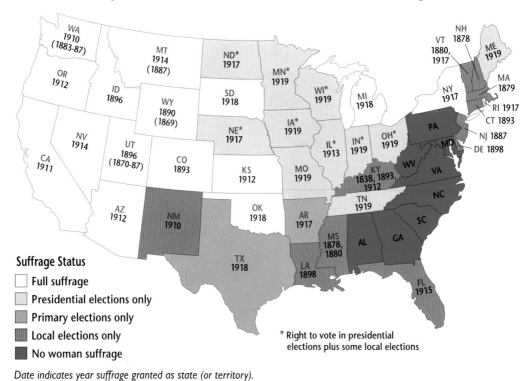

Suffrage Status

- ☐ Full suffrage
- ☐ Presidential elections only
- ☐ Primary elections only
- ☐ Local elections only
- ☐ No woman suffrage

* Right to vote in presidential
elections plus some local elections

Date indicates year suffrage granted as state (or territory).

Before 1920, a woman's right to vote was determined by state and local laws. Different regions were more or less supportive of suffrage. Women in the South had the fewest opportunities to vote. Women from western states gained some of the earliest voting rights. Women had to win over the support of male voters and lawmakers before most laws were changed.

actions at polling places, such as shortages of ballots, rigged vote counts, and undocumented voters. Sometimes suffragists celebrated victories only to watch them be taken away later by the courts.

Paul and her supporters persisted in their push for a federal amendment. Meanwhile the members of NAWSA, in the face of so many state defeats, wanted new leadership. They asked long-term member Carrie Chapman Catt to take charge of their organization. Catt was a veteran of Idaho's successful referendum of 1896 and had even led NAWSA briefly after Anthony's death. Now she agreed reluctantly to return to NAWSA's helm, even though it meant setting aside her work on the New York State campaign for suffrage.

In the fall of 1916, Catt proposed a Winning Plan for gaining woman suffrage. It broke down the 48 states into four categories and assigned each one with a task in what she said would be a "red-hot, never-ceasing campaign." States with full woman suffrage would be pressured to support a federal amendment. States with a hope of passing suffrage referenda would proceed with those fights. States where referenda were unlikely to pass would seek partial suffrage, as Illinois had done. Southern states, where even that goal was unrealistic, would seek the right to vote in presidential primaries.

Catt predicted that her Winning Plan would succeed by April 1922. She warned that "those who enter on this task, should go prepared to give their lives and fortunes for success." She insisted that the plan be kept secret, like a battle plan, to preserve its element of surprise. Catt demanded that at least 36 state chapters sign on as "armies," because that many states would be needed later to ratify an amendment. (Even more than 36 signed up for the plan.) She instructed her troops to take on federal lobbying in addition to their state work. Forces were instructed to "keep so much 'suffrage noise' going all over the country that neither the enemy nor friends will discover where the real battle" was occurring.

Catt unveiled her Winning Plan during a private meeting with leaders at a NAWSA convention. Later, President Wilson (unaware of her recent "war council") addressed all of the convention delegates. "I have not come to ask you to be patient, because you have been," said the President. But, he added, "you can afford a little while to wait." Former NAWSA president Anna Howard Shaw responded for the group by saying: "We have waited so long, Mr. President, for the vote—and we had hoped it might come in your administration." Then the entire audience stood up to emphasize this plea.

Catt sought one million dollars to fund her Winning Plan and raised most of it on the spot. Additional support came with a two-million-dollar

"A female creature, queer and quaint, Who longs to be just what she ain't We cannot efface— we can't forgive her— We love her still— the stiller the better."

–NELLY GORDON
February 4, 1916
poem sent to Alice Paul's suffragists
from an antisuffragist in Georgia

When President Woodrow Wilson appealed during the election year of 1916 for women to "be patient" about suffrage, NAWSA members reacted with restraint. In contrast, Alice Paul urged women with voting rights to cast ballots against the President and his Democratic Party. One hundred women "voiced" this idea at a presidential campaign stop in Chicago (above). Offended spectators attacked the group in a foreshadowing of coming events. (Wilson won his reelection bid.)

bequest for "the cause of woman suffrage" from Miriam F. Leslie, publisher of *Leslie's Weekly*. At last there was a comprehensive, organized, well-financed strategy in place. One of NAWSA's state leaders observed: "For the first time our goal looked possible of attainment in the near future."

One dark spot for some at the end of 1916 was the death of Inez Milholland, the horse-riding herald of 1913. Milholland, already in poor health, had collapsed during a speaking tour arranged by Alice Paul. She died ten weeks later. Her final public words became a rallying cry for radical suffragists: "President Wilson, how long must this go on—no liberty?" In early January 1917, Paul and 300 others asked the President to honor Milholland's death

by supporting woman suffrage. Wilson's chilly refusal stunned Harriot Stanton Blatch. What more could women do? she wondered. "We can't organize bigger and more influential deputations. We can't organize bigger processions," she complained. "We have to take a new departure."

Paul and her associates plotted a "new departure" from a new location on Lafayette Square. The White House stood nearby their headquarters, just across Pennsylvania Avenue. They had a new neighbor, too. As part of the Winning Plan, Catt had established Suffrage House in a 26-room mansion just six blocks from the White House. Its presence advertised that NAWSA was committed to a federal amendment, too. Now there were two suffrage groups at work in the U.S. capital. They may not have shared the same battle plans, but they had the same goal: the passage of a constitutional amendment granting women the right to vote.

PROTEST

"Mr. President, what will you do for woman suffrage?"

WHEN A DOZEN SUFFRAGISTS first mounted a picket line in front of the White House, Alice Paul knew just how they should look and behave. The women were to be "silent sentinels." Instead of calling out their demands to President Woodrow Wilson, they would write them on cloth banners for him—and everyone else—to see.

Alice Paul's radical suffragists took up this "new departure" battle plan on January 10, 1917. Four women hoisted cloth panels bearing two questions. One set of banners echoed Inez Milholland's final public plea: "How long must women wait for liberty?" The second pair asked, in matching block letters: "Mr. President, what will you do for woman suffrage?" Eight other pickets, or protesters, carried poles displaying the tricolor standard of their organization—panels of purple, white, and golden yellow cloth. Everyone wore tricolor sashes across their chests. "We always tried to make our lines as beautiful as we could," recalled Paul years later. "Our banners were really beautiful."

Pickets returned to their posts almost daily for the rest of the year. In the beginning they observed special occasions (such as Susan B. Anthony's

In the early weeks of White House picketing, suffrage supporters brought the women flowers, hot coffee, heated bricks to stand on (left), and outdoor gear like mittens, rubber boots, and raincoats. Volunteers maintained their vigil in any weather. The pickets practiced civil disobedience and nonviolent resistance decades before such techniques gained widespread use during the movement for African-American civil rights at midcentury.

birthday) and celebrated themes (for example, patriotism). Volunteers gathered for College Day (representing over a dozen schools), State Days (starting with Maryland), and Women Voters' Day (for women with state voting rights). Other women rallied to promote their careers as teachers, laborers, doctors, nurses, and lawyers.

Eventually as many as 2,000 women, representing more than half of the states in the Union, took turns picketing. They were as young as 19 and as old as 80. Many were college educated. About half were unmarried. Countless were self-supporting. With occasional exceptions—such as African-American suffragist Mary Church Terrell—they were white.

————— ★ —————

"How is it that people fail to see our fight as part of the great American struggle for democracy?"

—ALICE PAUL
November 27, 1917

Often the women were descendants of Quakers, abolitionists, and other reformers. Some were regulars, like Doris Stevens, who recalled how easy it was to daydream: "When *will* that woman come to relieve me?" Other pickets volunteered on a whim while visiting the city from elsewhere in the U.S. or abroad—some even while honeymooning.

Picketing the White House was so unheard of in 1917 that no one knew quite how to react. At first, Woodrow Wilson tipped his hat to the women when he passed. He instructed White House guards to offer them coffee. (The protesters politely declined it.) Newspaper reports were good-natured, even humorous. Wilson's patience with the pickets had worn thin by the time of his second Inauguration two months later. A thousand delegates from Paul's newly organized National Woman's Party celebrated the occasion on March 4 with a "grand picket." In those years citizens could still drop by and visit the President, but this battalion found the White House gates locked.

Despite the setback and wet, cold weather, Vida Milholland (sister of the fallen Inez) led the group in a march around the fenced grounds. "Mr. President, how long must women wait for liberty?" read Vida's golden banner. She and the women who followed fought with the wind to keep

Suffragists ignored poor weather and gathered for a "grand picket" on March 4, 1917. Spectators lined the streets to watch as women of all ages marched for two hours around the White House in a drenching rain.

their flags erect as they circled the White House four times. Finally the pickets observed Wilson's car leaving the property. The President and his wife drove past "as if the long line of purple, white, and gold was invisible," observed Doris Stevens. Apparently offers of free coffee were over.

At that point more than a dozen countries were already engaged in the conflict that would become known as World War I. No doubt President Wilson was more concerned with the possibility of U.S. involvement in this fight than with the pleas of woman suffragists. By early April, he felt compelled to ask Congress to declare war on Germany. "The world must be made safe for democracy," he insisted. "We shall fight for the things which we have always held nearest to our hearts—for democracy, for the right of those who submit to authority to have a voice in their own governments."

The U.S. entry into World War I prompted most suffragists to set aside work on enfranchisement, just as they had done during the Civil War. They worked with the Red Cross, took jobs in military supply factories, and filled in for departing troops. Some activists divided their time between war work and suffrage. Alice Paul did not. Her National Woman's Party adopted a "votes-for-women-first" policy: By supporting suffrage ahead of war work, they proclaimed, "the organization serves the highest interests of the country."

Paul reprinted the President's call for democracy on challenging—and, for Wilson, embarrassing—new banners. Surely U.S. women had the right "to have a voice in their own government," too. What better symbol than the right to vote? "Our military strategy was based on the military doctrine of concentrating all one's forces on the enemy's weakest point," recalled suffragist Doris Stevens. This point was "the inconsistency between a crusade for world democracy and the denial of democracy at home."

Armed with a seemingly endless supply of banners (and volunteers),

"America is not a democracy," challenged the "Russian Banners" of the National Woman's Party in June 1920. "Tell our government that it must liberate its people before it can claim free Russia as an ally" in World War I. The words provoked onlookers to destroy the banners.

Paul's "army" picketed not only at the White House but outside the U.S. Capitol, as well. Now, however, the growing nationalism of wartime made such protests seem, as reported in newspapers, "unwomanly," "unpatriotic," "dangerous," "undesirable," even "treasonable."

By late June, grumbling had escalated into violence. On the 20th, Russian envoys visited the White House to plan their strategy as allies for the war. Pickets greeted them with new banners. Their texts noted that Russian women had recently won the right to vote (during a national revolution), but 20 million American women still could not.

When the "Russian Banners" reappeared the next day, spectators tore the unpatriotic messages from their poles. Not for the first or last time in U.S. history, free speech became less important than national loyalty during wartime. Newspaper publishers made a "gentleman's agreement" to minimize their coverage of the challenging pickets; perhaps decreased publicity would prompt the protests to stop. The chief of police warned Paul that future pickets faced arrest. "We have picketed for six months without interference," observed Alice Paul. "Has the law been changed?" No, he said, "but you must stop it." She did not.

The first arrests of suffrage pickets began on June 22, 1917. By month's end, 27 women had been apprehended for "causing a crowd to gather and thus obstructing traffic." Six of them were tried and convicted. Their options: pay a $25 fine or spend three days in the District Jail. The women—including three teachers and a nurse—refused to pay. They became the first suffragists to serve prison terms in the United States.

By July, Paul's National Woman's Party had more provocative banners. "Governments derive their just power from the consent of the governed," read the text on the Fourth of July, quoting from the Declaration of Independence. Ten more women were arrested and jailed for three days. On July 14, Bastille Day (French independence day), banners repeated the French demand for "Liberty, Equality, Fraternity." This time suffragists faced a new challenge—a mob.

Suffragist Inez Haynes Irwin recorded the pattern of a forming mob. There was "the slow growth of the crowds; the circle of little boys who gathered about [pickets] first, spitting at them, calling them names, making personal comments; then the gathering gangs of young hoodlums who encouraged the boys to further insults; then more and more crowds; more and more insults; the final struggle. . . . Sometimes that crowd would edge nearer and nearer until there was but a foot of smothering, terror-fraught space between them and the pickets."

Suffragists learned to recognize regular foes on the picket line. This photo captures the faces (looking at camera) of four of the most persistent attackers. The growing number of servicemen massing in the nation's capital became regular participants in mob action. Sailors competed to win a daily five-dollar bet to see who could steal the greatest number of banners. The man at right won most often.

On July 14 police were more concerned with disciplining the suffragists than with the behavior of the mob. They arrested 16 women, including grandmothers, the descendant of a signer of the Declaration of Independence, and suffrage leaders Lucy Burns and Vida Milholland. In an effort to discourage more picketing, the judge pronounced a harsh sentence: $25 fines or 60 days at the Occoquan Workhouse in Virginia. The women went to jail. The unexpectedly severe punishment created an uproar among family members and supporters. Wilson felt forced to pardon the prisoners three days later.

A growing mob of spectators, mostly male, trailed after pickets on their way to protest their lack of voting rights at the White House on Bastille Day, July 14, 1917. Pickets march forward with courage and cloth, seemingly oblivious of shouts from the threatening crowd.

Tensions eased briefly, and pickets resumed without arrest. Then, on August 14, a new banner provoked unrest. It called the President "Kaiser Wilson," using the title of Germany's leader, Kaiser Wilhelm II. The banner accused Wilson of expressing sympathy for disenfranchised Germans while ignoring the 20 million women who could not vote in the U.S. "Take the beam out of your own eye," it challenged.

The so-called Kaiser Banner, with its criticism of the commander in chief, inflamed a gathering mob. Soldiers and sailors, young boys and grown men attacked the pickets. They tore at the women's banners, sashes, and clothes. They wrenched away banner poles, broke them, and used them as weapons. Police officers stood by or even helped, as the women were harassed and kicked. They even arrested men who tried to assist the women. The mob followed the retreating women back to their nearby headquarters. Police watched as men attempted to storm the building using a ladder and fired shots at it.

Alice Paul picketed early in 1917 (often dictating to a secretary from the picket line). She was so valuable at headquarters, though, that colleagues later discouraged her from protesting in public. They didn't want to lose her to a lengthy jail term. By fall she insisted on taking that risk in order to promote their cause.

Picketing and violence continued for two more days; over 200 banners were destroyed in the process. Finally, on August 17, police took control of the scene by arresting pickets (not mob members!). Six women, including Lucy Burns, were sentenced to pay ten dollars or serve 30 days at the Occoquan Workhouse. This time there were no pardons. The outspoken Burns drew the added punishment of solitary confinement.

Continued protests in September put dozens of others in jail, some with terms as long as six months. Stiffer penalties did not deter the pickets. "So long as you send women to jail asking for freedom, just so long will there be women willing to go to jail," observed one regular protester.

Lawmakers seemed not to notice their determination. National Woman's Party suffragists had renamed the proposed amendment the "Susan B. Anthony amendment." Despite prewar promises, it had not seen action in the U.S. Senate since 1914 or in the House since 1915. When Congress prepared to adjourn in October without acting on suffrage, however, an outraged Paul set aside her desk work for a march to the picket line (and almost certain arrest). She knew there would be less lobbying to do with lawmakers away, and she might gain more attention for her cause by going to jail. It didn't take long to get there. "Dear Mother: I have been sentenced today to seven months imprisonment," Paul wrote home on October 22. "Please do not worry. It will merely be a delightful rest. With love, Alice." Within days Paul was put into solitary confinement at the District Jail.

Dozens of pickets protested Paul's treatment and were arrested, too. On November 14, 33 of them were sentenced to Occoquan Workhouse for anywhere from six days to six months.

President Wilson had a public relations nightmare on his hands. At first he (and almost everyone else) had dismissed the militant suffragists as crazed. But—with mob violence, so many arrests, and lengthy jail sentences—public opinion was shifting. Letters to Wilson supporting the suffragists began to far outnumber those against them. Media support was growing, too. "These women have raised neither hand nor voice," wrote one female reporter who eventually stood on the picket line herself and was arrested. "They speak no word and do not attempt to defend themselves if attacked," she explained. Others accused President Wilson of tyranny for trying to subdue free speech.

Now it was the government's turn to be criticized and embarrassed. After all, Wilson himself had provided most of the text for the banners of the silent sentinels. How *could* the nation claim to fight for democracy abroad when it failed to treat citizens democratically at home?

★

"Then I saw the force that was sending those banners forward. . . . The leader [was] a woman frail, and slight, and very pale, her eyes and face really lit with exaltation of purpose."

—PAULINE JACOBSON
October 13, 1917
describing Alice Paul in her report
for the *Suffragist*

47

PRISON

"We worried Woody Wood as we stood."

THE LEADERS OF NAWSA did not like Alice Paul's pickets. "No one can feel worse than I do over the foolishness of their picketing the White House," commented Anna Howard Shaw, past president of the suffrage organization. Carrie Chapman Catt agreed. Such behavior seemed "unwise and unprofitable to the cause." What good could come from offending the very politicians who were needed to support a woman suffrage amendment?

Catt sought to remain on amiable terms with President Woodrow Wilson by distancing herself from the increasingly radical Alice Paul. In contrast to Paul's National Woman's Party, Catt's NAWSA agreed early in 1917 to "pledge the loyal support" of its two million members toward any war effort. Many women, including Catt, continued their work on the Winning Plan, as well.

Although NAWSA and the National Woman's Party approached their work from very different perspectives, they did share the same final goal.

In 1917 NAWSA president Carrie Chapman Catt (front right, wearing suffrage white) marched in the final New York City suffrage parade accompanied by former president Anna Howard Shaw (far left, in her black academic gown) and 20,000 other participants. Women gained the right of state suffrage there soon after. That year Catt's Winning Plan brought more state victories than defeats for the first time ever. Women earned an influence in nearly half of all electoral college votes as a result.

A large crowd gathered to watch the July 4, 1917, arrests of suffrage pickets. Women were carted away, banners and all. Mischievous boys would call out a cheeky answer to the banner question: "How long must women wait for liberty?" "Three months you'll be waiting," they suggested—three months in the Occoquan Workhouse.

As a result, even though the two groups operated independently of one another, the efforts of one organization often benefited the other, at least indirectly. Lawmakers who might have been reluctant to discuss the possibility of woman suffrage in earlier years, for example, were relieved to entertain visits by the more subdued NAWSA members. These suffragists seemed charming and quaint in contrast to the more militant style of Paul's recruits. At the same time the more radical National Woman's Party was able to keep suffrage a visible issue during 1917 in a way that Catt's workers could not given their dual service to the war effort.

There was little communication between the two organizations, however, and no behind-the-scenes collaboration for the cause. When others began to criticize the Wilson government for its handling of National Woman's Party pickets, Catt neither condemned the women's imprisonment nor questioned their treatment.

In all, more than 200 National Woman's Party pickets were arrested (often repeatedly) during the 1917 fight for suffrage. That year 106 of them served prison sentences. They were incarcerated at either the District Jail in the nation's capital or the Occoquan Workhouse in neighboring Virginia. These women might have been militant about suffrage, but otherwise most of them were ordinary citizens. One mother-daughter pair went to jail together. So did a trio of sisters. Several prisoners were mothers of as many as six children.

A sister, whose brother had died fighting in France, went to jail willing to perish herself, if necessary, to gain freedom for women. One young woman went to jail because her suffragist mother had "no son to fight for democracy abroad," and so she sent her daughter to "fight for democracy at home." One mother was jailed after protesting her lack of any say as a nonvoter in joining a war that had cost all her sons their lives.

Other "jailbirds," as they called themselves, were teachers, physicians, artists, a playwright, and an aviator. One woman in her 60s had been arrested years before. (Her offense? She had tried to vote in 1896.) Another was the daughter of an Army officer and the mother of three soldiers. Two were daughters of former congressmen. (By now there was one congresswoman: Jeannette Rankin. Rankin was newly elected from Montana, where she had led that state's successful fight for woman suffrage in 1914.)

> *"In prison or out, American women are not free. . . . Disfranchisement is the prison of women's power and spirit."*
>
> –KATHARINE ROLSTON FISHER
> Fall 1917
> National Woman's Party jailbird

Many spouses of suffragists—unlike Henry Stanton who fled town before the Seneca Falls Convention of 1848—were supportive of their militant wives. One newlywed husband joked that "it's got to be love at first sight, for you're not likely to get a second." Another husband, recovering from a stroke, told his wife he could "get along" without her while she went to jail. All spouses worried. At least one husband bailed an ailing wife out of jail, despite her wish to remain there.

Convicted pickets were transported from the District Courthouse to prison in the "Black Maria" wagons of the police force. Note the woman at right who still wears her tricolor suffrage sash from her day's march on the picket line.

Even on a good day, prison life was hard. Women at Occoquan Workhouse were issued uncomfortable clothing. Shoes were not only one-size-fits-all, for example, but interchangeable between feet. Blankets were washed once a year. The unfortunate suffragists arrived several months before the blankets were scheduled for their annual cleaning. Prisoners might be put on punishment rations of bread and water and denied the right to clean clothes. One woman went 11 days in the same garments. The women endured minimal sanitary conditions. A bucket might serve as "toilet"; real toilets were flushed at the whim of the guards.

Bloodhounds bayed outside the prison. Guards threatened to use their whipping post, mouth gags, and straitjackets inside. Rats fought in the shadows. The women were prohibited from talking at meals, which featured worm-infested grains and soups. Guards, who were male, denied the women any privacy. Prisoners were refused regular access to toothbrushes, combs, soap, and toilet paper. They were denied writing supplies and reading materials.

> *"I should be proud of the honor to die in prison for the liberty of American women."*
>
> –MARY NOLAN
> November 10, 1917
> upon her arrest at age 73

Suffrage prisoners toiled alongside other workhouse inmates at sewing, cleaning, and other tasks. When they could, suffragists taught one another foreign languages, offered other "classes," and sang songs. By taking turns singing verses, each inmate was able to signal to friends in neighboring cells that she was still all right. Sometimes the women composed a new song, with each prisoner adding lines in turns. "We worried Woody Wood as we stood," they sang in criticism of Woodrow Wilson. "Now, ladies, take the hint. Don't quote the President. Don't quote the President, as ye stand," concluded the song.

Conditions at the District Jail were as dismal as those at Occoquan. (Although there was no workhouse, rats were bold enough to invade jail cells at night.) By the fall of 1917 women at both facilities began calling themselves political prisoners. They insisted that politics, not criminal behavior, had landed them in jail. They protested their lack of access to legal counsel and complained about their living conditions. Those held at the workhouse refused to do any more prison labor.

Paul emphasized the injustice of the government's reaction to the pickets when she was arrested in late October. "I am being imprisoned not because I obstructed traffic, but because I pointed out to President Wilson the fact that he is obstructing the progress of justice and democracy at home while Americans fight for it abroad," she said at her trial. When she arrived at the District Jail soon after, officials secured the outspoken leader in solitary confinement. Paul, who weighed not even 100 pounds, grew weak on a diet of salt pork, bread, molasses—and no exercise. "However gaily you start out in prison to keep up a rebellious protest, it is nevertheless a terribly difficult thing to do," observed the suffrage leader, who had joked about finding a "delightful rest" in prison.

> ★
>
> *"I feel that every atom of American self respect within me has been outraged."*
>
> –ELIZABETH McSHANE
> recorded November 26, 1917
> a few days after being force-fed in prison

After two weeks, Paul and Rose Winslow, another weakened protester, were carried on stretchers to the prison hospital. The pair began a hunger strike, the first U.S. suffrage prisoners to do so. Prison officials responded by placing Paul in the psychiatric ward in an effort to prove her insane. Paul maintained her hunger strike—and her sanity—despite episodes of sleep deprivation, interrogation, and force-feeding. After a week, she was moved back to the hospital. When other suffragists at the District Jail heard of her hunger strike, they joined it.

At the same time, the 33 November pickets who had protested Paul's prison treatment were on their way to Occoquan Workhouse. The facility's staff sought to discourage further picketing by welcoming these new arrivals (ranging in age from 19 to 73) with what became known among suffragists as the "Night of Terror."

Vida Milholland peered between the bars of her District Jail cell after being arrested for picketing on the Fourth of July, 1917. Some 500 women were arrested and 168 were jailed during the final years of the fight for woman suffrage. Most of the prison terms were served during 1917. Some women escaped prison because charges against them were dropped. Others were prevented from going to prison by family or friends who insisted on paying their fines. A few women paid fines willingly to avoid jail.

Prison guards seemed crazed with rage when the women arrived on November 15. They manhandled the women to their cells, shoving, throwing, and knocking them down. They threatened the prisoners, twisted their arms, grabbed them by their necks, refused to treat injuries, and deprived them of access to bathrooms. When Lucy Burns tried to call a roll of the scattered prisoners, guards handcuffed her, arms raised, to the door of her cell for the rest of the night.

Many of the new prisoners took up hunger strikes in protest. Their days, like those of the women fasting at the District Jail, blurred together into a shadowy haze of nausea, fever, weakness, and fainting. Soon there was the added terror of force-feeding. Officials had already put Alice Paul and others at the District Jail on this regimen three times daily.

Elizabeth McShane, a former school principal, described the force-feeding process at Occoquan. A doctor poured a pint of cold milk mixed

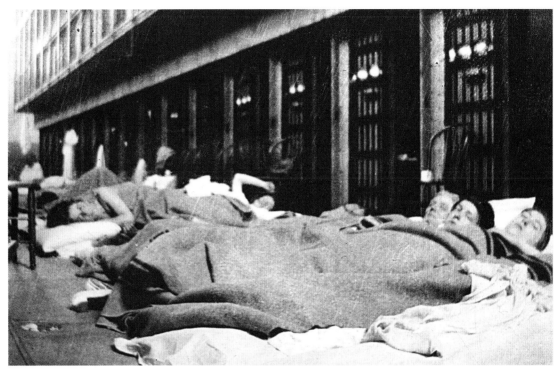

The "Night of Terror" reception given to arriving prisoners in Occoquan Workhouse in November 1917—combined with their subsequent hunger strikes—left the inmates weakened but nonetheless defiant. They rested on straw mats outside their cells. Jailers tried unsuccessfully to tempt the women to eat with special food treats (including fried chicken); later they force-fed them. One inmate recalled watching a prison rat carry away her uneaten rations.

with two raw eggs into a tube inserted down the throat. "Of course a stomach that has been unaccustomed to food for a week cannot take so much liquid cold, all in half a minute," explained McShane. The mixture went down so quickly that before the doctor "was half through, it began to come up, out of the corners of my mouth and down my neck until my hair was stiff with it. [I] tried to. . .check the flow for a second, but it poured on until all was finished. When he pulled the tube out, it was followed by a large part of the food. Thereupon the matron and he walked away, leaving me in that messy condition." Fellow inmate Lucy Burns, who had fought off force-feeding in England, could not be coerced into opening her mouth even with five people holding her captive. Her dose was poured through a feeding tube inserted into her nose.

The suffrage inmates were denied regular access to legal counsel and visitors, so they smuggled out secret accounts of their treatment with

Following their release from prison, Vida Milholland (center) and other former jailbirds performed prison songs and spoke around the country to raise national awareness about their cause. The women, sometimes dressed like prisoners, entertained crowds and made literature drops from the train they had chartered for their travels. They sought local support for suffrage that would influence national legislators to pass the Anthony amendment.

departing prisoners. (Some prisoners left because they had completed their sentences; others were bailed out by concerned family members.)

Confronted with mounting stories of brutality, President Wilson sent a prison commissioner to verify conditions firsthand. The man, assuming the President wanted to hear a positive story, reported that nothing was wrong in jail. Even the force-feedings were done cooperatively, he claimed. Although the record is inconclusive, Wilson seems to have knowingly tolerated at least some of the prison violence in an effort to discourage the embarrassing pickets.

Suffrage lawyers managed to arrange a hearing for the Occoquan prisoners before a Virginia judge on November 23. Reporters packed the courtroom and witnessed the "slender file of women, haggard, red-eyed, sick . . . [some of whom still] bore the marks of the attack of the 'Night of Terror.'" Many prisoners were so weak from days of hunger strikes that they stretched out on courthouse benches, unable to sit up.

If these women belonged in jail at all, their attorneys argued, then they should be held in the local District Jail, not in Virginia. The judge agreed. The women had been charged and convicted of crimes in Washington, D.C. Any sentences had to be carried out there, too.

Within five days Wilson had pardoned the suffragists from even this fate. It was too difficult—and unpopular—to keep the women in the small local jail, particularly with dozens of them now on hunger strikes. Alice Paul's seven-month jail sentence ended after five weeks. She had spent three of them on a hunger strike.

Convinced they had been jailed without reason, the women sued the government for damages and sought to have their records cleared. What law had they broken? Why was it all right to picket early in 1917 but not later on? Why were they charged with "obstructing sidewalk traffic" when it was the gathering mobs who actually disrupted the scene? Why hadn't the police disciplined violent crowds? Weren't their own arrests simply illegal efforts by the government to silence their peaceful protest? Eventually the Appeals Court agreed and overturned all of their arrests and convictions.

In early December the National Woman's Party honored its jailbirds by presenting each one with a commemorative silver pin (above). "A flame of rebellion is abroad among women," announced Alva Belmont, chair of the meeting.

★

Did the silent sentinels bring women closer to suffrage? Although Congress adjourned in 1917 without acting on the Anthony amendment, lawmakers could not dodge the measure much longer. Protesters had for the first time kept suffrage on the national agenda during wartime. They had increased public sympathy for their cause, too. Their efforts, combined with the state suffrage successes of NAWSA, were tipping the balance in favor of giving the vote to women.

★ ★ ★ ★ ★ ★

CHAPTER SIX

1918 – 1919

ACTION

"This old fight here unwon"

WHEN CONGRESS RECONVENED early in January 1918, President Woodrow Wilson finally gave suffragists what they wanted—his support. On January 9, he declared himself in favor of woman suffrage. His gratitude for the work women were doing for the war effort influenced his decision to speak. Without a doubt his interest in avoiding another year of unseemly protests and arrests was another factor. The divergent but parallel strategies of Carrie Chapman Catt and Alice Paul had worked.

The next day—exactly one year after silent sentinels had started their pickets—the House of Representatives began considering the Susan B. Anthony amendment. During the heated debate some members shouted comments like "They did it!" and "Well they got him!" regarding the influence militant suffragists seemed to have had on Woodrow Wilson.

Then representatives cast their second vote in three years on a federal amendment for woman suffrage. This time the measure passed, 274 votes to 136. There was one "yes" vote to spare. Suffragists left the chamber

Suffragists gathered by a statue of General Lafayette near their headquarters in Washington, D.C., for a series of protests beginning in August 1918. These demonstrations, and others the next year, provoked varied reactions depending on the tone of the protest and the makeup of the crowd. Sometimes police and mobs were as hostile as ever. Plenty of banners were wrenched from suffragists and turned into weapons. Other times some onlookers applauded while others shouted insults. Supportive crowds might offer spontaneous donations to the cause.

Nina Allender (left) drew hundreds of cartoons about woman suffrage. Her work in *The Suffragist* weekly of the National Woman's Party helped rally support from members nationwide for the ratification fight. This newspaper, founded in 1913, was the rival of the weeklies issued by NAWSA.

gallery singing a hymn of gratitude. The women were especially appreciative of five prosuffrage representatives who had ignored serious health issues in order to vote. For example, Frederick Hicks, a Republican from New York State, left his dying wife, at her request, so he could support suffrage. (She died while he was away.)

Approval by the House was half the battle. Next came the Senate. Rules required the amendment to pass both chambers in the same legislative session. With Congress set to adjourn in March 1919, that left 14 months for senators to act. Both NAWSA and the National Woman's Party expected swift success. Carrie Chapman Catt was so optimistic she ordered a new dress for the ratification campaign that would follow Senate approval. Alice Paul suspended militant protests. Preliminary tallies showed the amendment 11 votes shy of Senate passage. With the new support of the President, suffragists expected it would be easy to recruit the needed votes. They were wrong.

Catt who was based at NAWSA's New York headquarters, made dozens of trips to Washington, D.C., to lobby senators for support. Scores of other suffragists did the same, both from her organization and from the National Woman's Party. Both groups asked recruits beyond the nation's capital to stir up local pressure in the home states of wavering senators. One suffragist described the influence Alice Paul had on her field workers: "That sense we had of her—brooding and hovering back there in Washington—always gave us courage; always gave us the physical strength to do the things we did and the mental strength to make the decisions we made."

Senate support did grow, but by mid-summer projected tallies were still two votes short. By then neither the suffragists nor Wilson (who was preoccupied with winning World War I) seemed able to convert any other "no" or "maybe" votes into "yes" ones. Alice Paul returned to a familiar weapon: her arsenal of protest banners.

On August 6 National Woman's Party suffragists staged a demonstration in the "front yard" they shared with the President: Lafayette Square. They gathered at the base of a statue honoring Marquis de Lafayette, the French general who aided the U.S. during the Revolutionary War. No sooner did women speak than police began to arrest them. Officers apprehended Alice Paul even though she only watched empty-handed with other bystanders. In no time 48 suffragists (half of the protesters) were whisked off to court. These were the first protests and arrests since the previous November. Others continued in the following days.

By this time all of the 1917 suffrage arrests and convictions had been overturned. Prosecutors struggled over how to charge these new detainees.

★

"To deny women the vote longer in any part of the country makes of our war aims a travesty and a lie. It offers vindication to the German claim that America pretends to lofty aims but they are mere talk!"

—CARRIE CHAPMAN CATT
June 22, 1918

What laws could the women be charged with breaking? They settled on the flimsy complaints of "holding a meeting in public grounds" and "climbing on a statue." The convicted women refused to pay any fines. "It is quite enough to pay taxes when you are not represented," observed Mary Winsor at her August 15 trial. She was not about to "pay a fine if you object to this arrangement." Thus the judge was forced to repeat the pattern of 1917—send the women to jail. This time he handed out shorter sentences (10 to 15 days) so that hunger strikes could not be so dramatic.

> ★
>
> *"As a disfranchised class we feel we are not subject to the jurisdiction of this court and therefore we refuse to take part in its proceedings."*
>
> –ALICE PAUL
> August 15, 1918
> commenting to the judge
> during a trial of suffrage pickets

Authorities reopened a condemned workhouse at the District Jail in order to accommodate the overflow of inmates. The facility featured unhealthful water, damp cells, air tainted with sewer gas, and—of course—rats. The inmates declared themselves political prisoners and went on hunger strikes. Public outcry over the conditions forced officials to release them after five days.

When senators threatened on September 16 to recess without voting on the Anthony amendment, suffragists returned to Lafayette Square. This time they brought matches. That same day Wilson had pledged to "urge the passage of the amendment by an early vote." A protester held a torch to a copy of Wilson's words and proclaimed: "The torch which I hold symbolizes the burning indignation of the women who for years have been given words without action."

Perhaps influenced by this protest, senators agreed to vote on the amendment after all. With defeat seeming certain, Carrie Chapman Catt urged Wilson to visit Capitol Hill. The President did. "We have made partners of the women in this war," he said in the Senate chamber. "Shall we admit them only to a partnership of suffering and sacrifice and toil and not to a partnership of privilege and of right?" he asked. Wilson's last-minute plea fell flat. When senators voted on October 1, they failed to pass the

Vida Milholland (center, holding flag), and other former jailbirds received warmer welcomes in the later years of Prison Special train tours than had earlier travelers. "Some say we ought to be *tarred and feathered*," reported a suffragist during a southern tour in November 1917. The Secret Service, always suspicious of National Woman's Party activities, shadowed their movements often.

amendment—as expected—by two votes. Most opposition came from the suffrage-wary South. "There are some differences between men and women that were ordained by the Almighty," argued a Democratic senator from the former slave state of Missouri during the floor debate.

For once Alice Paul and Carrie Chapman Catt chose the same plan of action. With Election Day just weeks away, they mobilized to defeat anti-suffrage senators and support prosuffrage candidates. At the same time Paul pressured the Senate to reconsider its vote; she initiated six weeks of picketing on Capitol Hill. Neither strategy worked. The net result of election gains and losses left suffragists two votes short, again. And the Senate recessed November 21 without reconsidering woman suffrage. Time was running out. When Congress reconvened in January, its members would meet for only a few weeks.

Suffragists from the National Woman's Party unveiled a new provocative banner when they kindled their perpetual watch fire at the White House on January 1, 1918. The women fed the fire by smuggling kerosene-soaked logs under their coats to the site. "Everything and everybody smelled of kerosene," recalled a participant. The logs proved remarkably flammable. Suffragists kept the fire alight for weeks despite wet weather and regular attempts by the police and mobs to put it out.

November 11, 1918, brought the truce that ended World War I. The next month Wilson sailed to France to participate in the peace talks. National Woman's Party suffragists observed his departure with a torch-lit ceremony in Lafayette Square on December 16. Olympia Brown tossed Wilson's latest speech into a flame-filled cauldron. "I have fought for liberty for 70 years," said the 84-year-old suffrage ally of Susan B. Anthony. "I protest against the President leaving our country with this old fight here unwon."

The good news by the end of 1918 was that women in 15 of the nation's 48 states now had full suffrage rights. Catt's "Winning Plan" had brought victories in Michigan (after a 44-year fight), South Dakota, and Oklahoma. Those 15 states were joined by 6 others where women had some form of presidential suffrage.

On January 1, 1919, Alice Paul began a new form of protest. She established a perpetual watch fire in front of the White House where suffragists could burn the President's speeches on democracy "as fast as he made them in Europe." Paul was among those arrested and released that day; she returned to help guard the fire through a rain-filled night.

By the end of the month, dozens of suffragists had been arrested for this action (Paul twice). They were charged with "building a bonfire on a public highway between sunrise and sunset." The punishment: $5 or 5 to 10 days in the District Jail. The women went to jail. (The facility had been cleaned since their stay in 1917, but rats still "ran about in hordes.") These protesters were joined by dozens of other suffragists who had been arrested for applauding during the trials. Virtually everyone went on a hunger strike.

President Wilson, aware of the watch fire burning at home, began pressuring antisuffrage Democrats to change their votes. One replied he would never support suffrage until Paul's protesters "stopped making fools of themselves." But, on February 2, 1919, a senator from South Carolina announced he would vote for suffrage. The Anthony amendment was one vote away from passing, and a new Senate vote was set for February 10.

★

"We kept a list of [determined anti-suffrage senators] and we sent to them any woman who was wavering on suffrage. It never failed to make her a strong suffragist."

–MAUD YOUNGER
March 2, 1919

The day before the vote, militant suffragists gathered to burn a drawing of Wilson in their flaming cauldron. Police arrested 39 of the 100 participants. They had to commandeer nearby automobiles to haul away the bumper crop of prisoners. The judge tired of trying so many offenders. After sentencing the 26th woman to five days at the District Jail's reopened workhouse, he set the remaining suffragists free.

As expected, the Senate vote on February 10 came up short by one man. (The first woman would not be elected to the Senate until 1932.) With the

President set to return home from France on February 24, Alice Paul traveled to Boston and organized a welcoming protest. This dockside demonstration led to 21 arrests for "loitering more than seven minutes." These women received the final prison sentences of the woman suffrage fight: eight days in the Charles Street Jail. Several began hunger strikes. Two former college roommates were reunited as cell mates during a stay that was cut short by an unsolicited bailout. All of the jailbirds from 1918-19 earned prison pins, too.

After Anna Howard Shaw turned over the leadership of NAWSA to Carrie Chapman Catt, she continued to endorse woman suffrage through numerous speeches (such as the one advertised above). Cross-country travels for this cause and for war-related issues weakened her health. She died on July 2, 1919, shortly after Congress passed the Anthony amendment.

★

Jail time wasn't always the final consequence of suffrage work. Some protesters, such as schoolteacher Margaret Fotheringham, lost their jobs (for failing to return to work on time). Munitions worker Ruth Scott was evicted from her apartment. Betsy Reneau was disowned by her father in a letter sent to President Wilson. Effie Boutwell Main was divorced by a husband on charges of disgrace. (Other suffragists with disapproving husbands were forbidden from protesting at all.)

Congress adjourned its session on March 3, 1919, without reconsidering the Anthony amendment. The House support of 1918 would no longer count. Now both bodies of Congress would need to pass the amendment before it could be considered for ratification by the states.

The next day members of the National Woman's Party staged what would become the last demonstration to provoke a violent reaction during the fight for woman suffrage. They met in New York City with plans to stage a watch fire outside the Metropolitan Opera House where President Wilson was giving a speech. Alice Paul was among those who marched from the organization's local headquarters to the site. As banner-waving suffragists approached, "two hundred policemen in close formation rushed us with unbelievable ferocity," participant Doris Stevens later recalled. "They spoke not a word but beat us back with their clubs with such cruelty as none of us had ever witnessed before."

The conflict lasted for hours, long enough for Paul and others to be arrested for "assaulting the police," released, and apprehended again. Soldiers and sailors joined in, not only at the demonstration, but back at headquarters, where they broke in and destroyed suffrage banners. Suffragists were dismissed without trial.

Later that month Carrie Chapman Catt participated in a previously planned "Jubilee Convention" for NAWSA members. The meeting celebrated the 50th anniversaries of its parent groups (the "National" and "American" woman suffrage associations). Members had hoped to be able to applaud the passage of the Anthony amendment, too. Catt, never idle, began planning what role her organization could play after the eventual granting of woman suffrage.

Two months later President Wilson, while back in Europe, recruited the missing vote for woman suffrage: a new senator from Georgia. He used his executive powers to call Congress into special session. (Otherwise lawmakers would not have met again for months.) Legislators convened on May 19. By May 21 the House had taken the required action of again approving the Anthony amendment. This time there were 42 "yes" votes to spare. The Senate held its fifth and final vote on June 4, 1919. With approval now certain, two other senators supported the amendment, so it passed with two extra votes.

It had taken from 1878 until 1919—41 years—for the Anthony amendment to be approved by Congress. The work in the nation's capital was finally done. Now the voting rights of women were up to the states.

> ★
>
> *"The right of citizens of the United States to vote shall not be denied or abridged by the United States or by any State on account of sex."*
>
> —19TH AMENDMENT

★ ★ ★ ★ ★ ★ ★

CHAPTER SEVEN

1 9 1 9 – 1 9 2 0

VICTORY

"Hurrah! And vote for suffrage. . ."

NO ONE EXPECTED THE ratification of the 19th Amendment to be easy. In fact, antisuffrage forces hoped they could defeat it. The U.S. Constitution required three-fourths of the states to ratify an amendment. With 48 states in the Union as of 1919, suffragists needed 36 of them to approve the change. If Antis could find just 13 states to side with them, the amendment would not become law.

NAWSA and the National Woman's Party were ready for battle. Carrie Chapman Catt had a veritable army of people (about two million) waiting for duty. Alice Paul's forces numbered as many as another 50,000. These "troops" were stationed at branch offices in most states and were well acquainted with local leaders.

Antis were ready, too. Their forces were particularly strong in southern states, where many whites saw woman suffrage as a threat to states' rights and their interest in white supremacy over African Americans. Although most prosuffrage Southerners supported the amendment, a few favored only state-controlled suffrage and actually campaigned against ratification.

Suffragists fanned out across the country during 1919 and 1920 to urge ratification of the Anthony amendment. Bundles of banners give this pair away as members of the National Woman's Party. They were headed to visit Republican presidential candidate Warren G. Harding in Marion, Ohio, and urge his support of suffrage. (*See photo pages 74–75 for a scene from their visit.*)

Swing states beyond the South—those that might go either way—included Connecticut, Delaware, New Jersey, New Hampshire, and Vermont. As with the antisuffrage South, none of these swing states permitted women to vote in statewide elections.

Timing for a ratification fight could not have been worse. All but a handful of state legislatures were out of session in June 1919. Many legislatures were not scheduled to reconvene until fall, or even the next year, because all their required work was completed. Suffragists knew they could not afford delays. The pro-woman sentiments from World War I might evaporate when President Wilson's term ended after the 1920 election. Plus, if the states acted quickly enough, women could vote in that election. Otherwise four years would pass before another presidential contest occurred.

Catt and Paul started their campaigns by telegraphing state governors. They urged governors to bring the amendment before their legislatures, in special session if necessary. They initiated a race to see which state could ratify the amendment first. (Wisconsin won the honor on June 10.) Another ten states ratified quickly, but by early fall the tally had grown to only 14 "yes" votes. Plus three southern states had rejected the amendment.

Picketing by Alice Paul (above) and others outside the Republican national convention in Chicago may have influenced party members to endorse the 19th Amendment as part of its 1920 election platform. Democrats made the same commitment when they met soon after.

★

Catt pulled out her ratification dress from 1918, restyled it, and headed off on an eight-week, 13-state tour promoting ratification. Even Alice Paul, usually encamped at her Washington, D.C., headquarters, traveled into the field that fall to aid an uncertain effort in Maine. She returned home victorious (though by only four votes). That gain permitted her to add another star to the purple, white, and gold "ratification banner" she had created to record state victories.

Some governors opposed the amendment and refused to call their legislatures into session. Others were reluctant to incur the extra expense of a special session. (In these cases, suffragists volunteered to handle clerical work, and they encouraged lawmakers to serve without pay.) In some states suffragists had closed local offices where women already had the vote; it took time to rekindle old support. Even with these challenges, by the end of 1919 the 19th Amendment had been approved by 22 states. No others had voted to oppose it.

Even as suffragists pushed for ratification of the national amendment, NAWSA members continued to implement the "Winning Plan" for state suffrage. By year's end women had gained the right to vote in presidential elections in eight more states. Now they had a voice in more than half of the nation's electoral college votes.

Catt urged her troops on with the ratification battle, too. Typical advice was her parting order to a veteran worker. "You thought you had a real job in Vermont—that was only a pleasure trip," she wrote the New Hampshire-bound recruit. "This is a job. Come through with your shield or upon it."

> ★
>
> *"The plan of the Antis is to find 13 states which they can hold out against ratification. They have been good enough to give us the list."*
>
> —CARRIE CHAPMAN CATT
> July 1, 1919

One woman actually worked herself to death for ratification. Like Inez Milholland, Aloysius Larch-Miller ignored ill health and kept a speaking engagement on behalf of suffrage. This ill-timed appearance in Oklahoma during early 1920 contributed to her death two days later.

Suffragists in West Virginia depended on State Senator Jesse Bloch to gain ratification there during March 1920. For five days they kept prosuffrage lawmakers from defecting to the Antis while Bloch, who was wintering in California, raced home to vote in a special legislative session. His tie-breaking vote brought the state ratification tally to 34. Suffragists needed only two more states for victory. Washington State became one of them later that month.

In late July 1920, 200 suffragists from the National Woman's Party converged on the residence of newly nominated Republican Party candidate Warren G. Harding to urge his support of woman suffrage. Harding endorsed the idea, as did his rival, the Democrat James Cox. Although the major political parties had offered little or no support of woman suffrage in earlier elections, now their candidates were eager to court the potential new voters who would materialize if one more state ratified the 19th Amendment.

NICE
COL.

Then the ratification momentum died.

Suffragists were running out of states. Out of 48 states, 6 had now rejected the amendment. Only seven states had yet to weigh in on the issue, and most of these lay in or near the antisuffrage South. Was there one left that would approve woman suffrage? Suffragists took this question to leaders of the Republican and Democratic Parties during their June 1920 presidential conventions. Later on they pressed the issue with the parties' respective candidates for President: Senator Warren G. Harding from Ohio and that state's governor, James M. Cox.

With fewer simultaneous ratification battles in process, it was easier for antisuffragists to concentrate their forces on the remaining skirmishes. Both groups—pro and anti, males and females alike—descended on Tennessee. The state's antisuffrage governor, who was up for reelection, knew a suffrage vote would hurt him at the polls. As a Democrat, though, he was pressured to act by national party members from President Wilson on down. Finally, on June 25, he announced he would call a special session—but not until August— *after* the state's Democratic primary (which he hoped to win).

> ★
>
> *"It would be a real service to the party and to the nation. . . for you to. . .call a special session of the legislature of Tennessee to consider the suffrage amendment. Allow me to urge this very earnestly."*
>
> –PRESIDENT WOODROW WILSON
> June 23, 1920
> telegram to the governor of Tennessee

Tennessee legislators convened on Monday, August 9; within days the prosuffrage Senate had approved the amendment 25 to 4. The fate of the amendment was up to the House. "We now have 35 ½ states," Carrie Chapman Catt wrote to a friend. "We are up to our last half of a state." Legislators who had just defeated the amendment in neighboring North Carolina urged Tennessee lawmakers to fight suffrage "to the last ditch, and then some." Fighting is just what members of the Tennessee

Antisuffragists rallied in Tennessee in an effort to defeat ratification of the woman suffrage amendment. Among those opposing suffrage were members of the Southern Women's League for the Rejection of the Susan B. Anthony Amendment. (Members wear the trademark red rose of antisuffragists; suffragists wore yellow flowers.) A Confederate veteran from the Civil War (center) joined in with the reminder that he had "'fought and bled' for Tennessee's States' Rights."

Ratification of the 19th Amendment

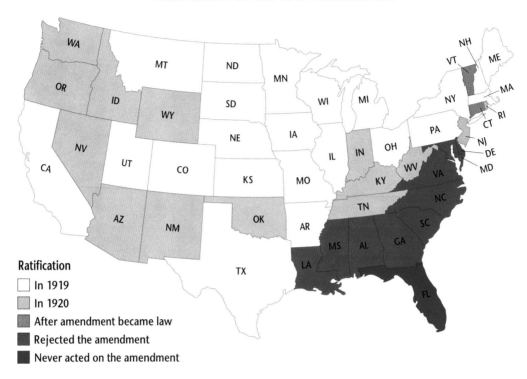

Ratification

- ☐ In 1919
- ◻ In 1920
- ▨ After amendment became law
- ◼ Rejected the amendment
- ◼ Never acted on the amendment

Although ratification of the 19th Amendment mirrored some earlier trends for voting rights—such as southern resistance to woman suffrage—not all prosuffrage states rushed to ratify the idea of federal voting rights for women. Almost half waited until 1920 before doing so. The U.S. territories of Alaska (where women had full suffrage) and Hawaii (where they had none) were excluded from the ratification process.

House did. Debates and delays continued there through five more days of late summer southern heat (long before air conditioning became commonplace).

Antis made good use of the passing time. "Never in the history of politics has there been such a force of evil," Catt later wrote. "Strange men and groups of men sprang up, men we had never met before in battle." She feared they were "buying votes," promising money to legislators who would vote against the amendment. Antis tried to sway lawmakers with liquor. (They had kept Tennessee senators up drinking the night before their vote until both pro- and antisuffrage legislators were drunk—and thus easier to influence.) Antis threatened prosuffrage legislators with financial ruin.

They promised to defeat their reelection bids. They encouraged lawmakers to leave town. (The night before the House vote, suffragists canvassed the railroad stations to assure needed voters stayed off departing trains).

Catt, who had witnessed ugly suffrage battles for three decades, was horrified. "Even if we win, we who have been here will never remember it with anything but a shudder," she wrote a friend. Catt spent two months in the state working to secure ratification support. Paul, too radical and unpopular to be helpful in Tennessee, stayed home. She recruited national leaders who might influence the state's legislators. Tennessee members of the National Woman's Party lobbied in their home state with efforts that paralleled those of NAWSA.

The amendment came to a vote in the Tennessee House on August 18. No one was sure which side would win. One prosuffrage legislator had to be brought from the hospital so he could voice his support. Another–torn between going home to be with a dying child or voting–leaped off a moving train so he could vote "yes." (Then he sped home by chartered train.)

★

"I [had] an opportunity such as seldom comes to a mortal man to free 17 million women from political slavery."

–HARRY BURN
August 1920
among the reasons
why he voted for ratification

The seventh member to vote during the roll call of legislators was Harry Burn, 24, the youngest member of the legislature. Two men had voted for ratification at that point, four against it. Burn was a Republican from an antisuffrage district in the mountains of east Tennessee. Neither pro- nor antisuffragists knew how he planned to vote that day, although all could see the antisuffrage red rose that adorned his jacket. Perhaps no one but Harry knew that he had a letter in his pocket from suffrage supporter Febb King Ensminger Burn, his mother.

"Hurrah! And vote for suffrage," Febb Burn had written her son. "I have been watching to see how you stood, but have noticed nothing yet. Don't forget to be a good boy and help Mrs. Catt put 'Rat' in Ratification."

Suffragists celebrated the passage of the 19th Amendment by ringing bells, blowing whistles, and throwing parties. Alice Paul stitched the 36th star on the banner she had used to tally state ratification votes. Then she unfurled it from the balcony of the National Woman's Party headquarters (above). Carrie Chapman Catt returned from the Tennessee ratification battleground to a welcome in New York City where women clapped so enthusiastically that they split the seams on their gloves. Supporters in Seneca Falls, New York, draped the memorial for the first woman's rights convention with a flag.

Burn cast his vote in favor of ratification. Without his help the vote would have tied. With it, the tally ended at 49 for, 47 opposed.

Afterward, Harry Burn gave several reasons why he had supported suffrage. One was his interest in bringing credit to his Republican Party for the amendment's passage. Then there was his mom. "I knew that a mother's advice is always safest for her boy to follow and my mother wanted me to vote for ratification."

One would think the fight for woman suffrage was over, but it was not. Antisuffragists tried to discredit the Tennessee vote. They attempted to overturn it and maneuvered to keep the governor from certifying the results. It took six days, more dickering in the legislature, and a decision from the state's supreme court before the Tennessee governor signed the "certificate of ratification" needed to prove the state's vote.

When the certificate reached Washington, D.C., in the early morning hours of August 26, the U.S. secretary of state was roused from his sleep, as he had requested. His haste may have been fueled as much by a reluctance to entertain rival suffragists at a more formal ceremony as by an eagerness to make the amendment official before anyone could try to stop him. After confirming the document was in order, he signed papers that declared the completed ratification of the 19th Amendment. His action ended the quest for women's voting rights that had begun 72 years and five weeks earlier at a hastily arranged meeting in Seneca Falls, New York. Other battles for equality loomed ahead, but now women had the power of the vote on their side.

Southern suffragists who had supported the 19th Amendment were disheartened that their new voting rights had come without more support from their own region. Eight southern states (plus the neighboring Delaware) rejected ratification; Florida failed to consider it. Many Southerners who had opposed the amendment bemoaned its passage and the federal imposition over states' rights that it represented.

Antisuffragists kept up challenges to the amendment even after it took effect. They tried to undermine the authenticity of the Tennessee vote. (This effort died after Connecticut's ratification in mid-September provided a backup vote to Tennessee's.) One more state—Vermont—went on to ratify the amendment the next year. Not until the Supreme Court upheld the legality of the 19th Amendment in two separate cases—the last one in February 1922—was woman suffrage assured.

"I feel much more respect for myself. . . and for all the human kind."

–GRACE EDWARDS

writing to Doris Stevens
following ratification of the
19th Amendment

⊚N ELECTION DAY IN 1919–the year before ratification of the 19th Amendment–about seven million U.S. women could vote in at least some of the elections in their states. By the election of 1920, 27 million women had full suffrage rights. Not all of these women chose to vote. Nine more presidential elections would come and go, over 36 years, before as many women went to the polls as men.

In 1920 not all women were permitted to vote, either. Many African-American women tried to register to vote, and some succeeded. But before the decade was over, racist southern officials had extended toward black women the same discriminatory tactics that kept black men from the polls. The rest of the country–from government leaders to newly enfranchised white suffragists–ignored this injustice. Voting remained a states' rights matter until the massive push for civil rights at mid-century. Even though the Voting Rights Act of 1965 effectively reopened the polls to African Americans, discrimination continues to surface.

Those women who did vote beginning in 1920 may have surprised

Although increasing numbers of women gained the right to mark ballots in the opening years of the 20th century (left), the 19th Amendment freed millions more to vote for the first time in the presidential election of 1920. Mothers brought an added voice to the polls for children and young adults. The voting age remained 21 until 1971 when it was lowered–with the ratification of the 26th Amendment–to 18.

suffragists and antisuffragists alike by continuing the voting trends of men. The old arguments that women voters would promote radical reform and upset the balance between political parties (if they favored only one of them) proved not to come true. Neither did the fears that voting would destroy womanliness and ruin marriages and families.

It's easy to be surprised by how long and difficult it was for women to earn the right to vote. Before men would share this power, many factors had to align with the persistence of suffrage demands: the increased role of women in the workplace, the proof that women with state suffrage rights could vote responsibly, the growing value of women as political party supporters, women's war service, and the renewed commitment to democracy fostered by World War I. Although these factors might have existed before at various times, they aligned with the greatest intensity when the battle finally was won.

"It was my rib, Eve," proclaimed this political cartoon shortly after ratification of the 19th Amendment. The same Democratic and Republican (G.O.P.) Parties that had been reluctant to support woman suffrage for more than half a century were eager to take credit for the granting of those rights in 1920. Each group hoped to gain an advantage over the other by winning the support of the new women voters.

★

Women abroad gained voting rights with varying speed. A number of countries beat the United States in the race for woman suffrage. These include Australia, Canada, Germany, Norway, and Poland. Some countries, such as Brazil, Great Britain, India, and Spain, expanded their franchise to women at about the same time as the U.S. Others—including Argentina, China, France, and Japan—waited to do so until the 1940s and another world war.

Some governments (such as Mexico, Nigeria, and Switzerland) delayed even longer to enfranchise women. Even today a few countries, such as Kuwait, deny women the right to vote.

In the spring of 1920 Carrie Chapman Catt transformed her old NAWSA army into a new organization, the League of Women Voters. She expected the League to encourage voter participation, educate nonvoters on their new responsibilities, and lobby for improved legislation. It would not favor any political party. Although the organization could have chosen to sponsor women candidates for election, it did not do so. A few former suffragists ran for office, but most of them heaved great sighs of relief, cast their ballots for men, and pursued other interests.

Catt, at 61 years old, left leadership of the League to others. She took up the cause of world peace and worked for that end until her death in 1947. Harriot Stanton Blatch devoted her final years to promoting world peace, too. She lived until 1940. Alice Stone Blackwell supported the League, among other causes, and wrote a biography of her mother, Lucy Stone; she died in 1950. Lucy Burns, who spent more time in U.S. jails than any other suffragist, withdrew from reform work. Her death came in 1966.

"The ballot is the symbol of a new status in human society, it is the greatest possible single step forward in the progress of women, but it does not in itself complete their freedom."

—THE SUFFRAGIST
September 1920

Alice Paul, the most mistreated suffrage jailbird, was only 35 years old when the 19th Amendment was ratified. She promptly went back to school and earned three degrees in law. Paul believed, as had Elizabeth Cady Stanton, that the right to vote was only a tool for gaining other rights. Even though women could vote, Paul realized they were not treated equally in marriage, at work, or by laws. Paul sought to correct this injustice with another amendment to the U.S. Constitution. She hoped this one would

A new generation of feminists joined Alice Paul in supporting her equal rights amendment (ERA) during the 1970s, but they did not always defer to its aging author on how to promote ratification. Paul predicted the measure would fail because of southern resistance and because younger feminists weren't aggressive enough in their efforts to

strengthen the rights of women, much as the 14th and 15th Amendments had expanded the rights granted to former slaves by the 13th Amendment.

Paul's idea became known as the equal rights amendment (ERA), and she worked for its passage for the rest of her life. The amendment, which Paul wrote, was first proposed to Congress in 1923 by the nephew of Susan B. Anthony, a member of the House of Representatives. Legislators reintroduced it (without ever acting on it) in every congressional session until 1970. Then it passed by a large margin in the U.S. House. It was approved by a similar majority in the Senate two years later. Only 23 legislators opposed it between the two chambers.

secure ratification. Women honored Paul after her death with a memorial parade (above) on August 26, 1977—the 57th anniversary of the ratification of the 19th Amendment. Parade participants wore white clothes in honor of the woman suffrage fight. Paul's ERA text filled one of the many banners carried in the march.

Within two years the ERA had been ratified by 33 states and needed only five more votes to become law. Lawmakers had set a limit to the ratification period, however, and the amendment still lacked three votes when that time and an additional extension expired in 1982. Efforts to revive the ERA have continued off and on ever since, but with no success as yet.

Alice Paul died in 1977 at the age of 92 knowing her ERA was unlikely to be ratified. Confused by illness at the end of her life, she mistook well-intentioned staff members at her nursing home for people who planned to force-feed her. She refused to eat and later died of heart failure. After passage of the 19th Amendment, membership dwindled in the National Woman's Party. Today the organization maintains a museum in Washington, D.C., from a headquarters near Capitol Hill, its home since 1929 and the place where I once met Alice Paul.

After ratification of the 19th Amendment, Alice Paul's National Woman's Party commissioned a "portrait monument" of founding suffragists (from left) Elizabeth Cady Stanton, Susan B. Anthony, and Lucretia Mott. (They chose to omit the less radical Lucy Stone.) They donated the statue to the U.S. government in 1921, and it was relegated to an obscure corner of the Capitol basement. Finally, in 1997, officials relocated the memorial to the Capitol Rotunda. The move followed renewed demands—including from the growing number of women elected to serve in Congress—that it be more prominently displayed.

★

It seems reasonable to expect the National Woman's Party to be remembered. It was, after all, the group that promoted the same techniques of nonviolent resistance later popularized by Martin Luther King, Jr., during the Civil Rights Movement. "When all suffrage controversy has died away, it will be the little army of women with their purple, white, and gold banners, going to prison for their political freedom, that will be remembered," suffragist Doris Stevens predicted.

However the silent sentinels and jailbirds were largely overlooked when historians recalled woman suffrage (if they did so at all). Sometimes historians simplified the suffrage story, telling about Elizabeth Cady Stanton and Susan B. Anthony but not Lucy Stone, or describing Catt's NAWSA but not Paul's National Woman's Party. Perhaps Paul's pickets seemed too radical, still too "unwomanly," to deserve

mention. Perhaps omitting their role allowed historians to avoid the uncomfortable subject of the government's attempts to suppress these protesters. Perhaps, at least when most historians were men, presenting the whole story may not have seemed that important. Not until the 1970s did a growing number of women historians begin to uncover the subtleties of the history of woman suffrage. Their work has yet to be fully integrated into the nation's popular understanding of the past.

What is the condition of voting rights in the U.S. today? Some restrictions remain on the franchise. Many states deny lifetime voting rights to convicted felons, for example, even years after they have served their sentences and returned to society. In general, though, there is broader suffrage today than at any prior time in the nation's history. That said, voter participation—the practice of actually voting—has rarely been lower. Presidential elections, which are always the most popular, rarely draw more than about half of eligible voters to the polls. Many citizens never even register to vote.

Voter turnout is lowest among the people who might stand to benefit from it the most, those with the least education, members of minorities, and the poor. Participation of these same voters can easily be manipulated, either by coaxing them to vote based on a special interest or by complicating their access to the polls. Old tricks of confusing ballots, inaccurate registration, and voter intimidation continue to resurface when they serve the interests of those in power.

Such abuses may arise from the nation's reluctant embrace of the right to vote. Suffrage was added to the Constitution piecemeal, over time. Suffrage rights, when they are gained, have not come easily. U.S. women earned the right to vote only after a hard-fought fight spanning generations. By understanding the history of suffrage gains, citizens may see that voting is not a right to be ignored or idly taken for granted.

At the close of the ratification battle in 1920, Carrie Chapman Catt observed: "This is a glorious and wonderful day." She noted that women were, at last, "not wards of the nation but free and equal citizens." Then she offered a reminder of the responsibility of voters then—and now, "Let us do our part to keep it a true and triumphant democracy."

Suffragists linked hands in a show of solidarity during one of the many parades that called attention to their demand for the right to vote.

★ PROFILES

SUSAN B. ANTHONY

BORN: Feb. 15, 1820, Adams, Mass. ◦— **DIED:** March 13, 1906, Rochester, N.Y., age 86

BACKGROUND: Susan Brownell Anthony was raised in a Quaker family in New York State. Although her first work was as a teacher, she soon turned to reform. She supported efforts to end slavery and discouraged the drinking of alcohol. Then she took up women's rights. Anthony turned down all wedding proposals because she believed marriage and family put limits on the independence of women.

CONTRIBUTION TO WOMAN SUFFRAGE: Freed of the distractions of family life, Anthony worked tirelessly for more than 50 years for the right of women to vote. She crisscrossed the nation seeking popular support for woman suffrage and lobbied state and federal legislators to write laws favoring votes for women. In 1872 she talked her way past her local voting registrar and cast a ballot for Ulysses S. Grant and his Republican Party. This challenge of the law led to her arrest and a highly publicized trial. Although she was convicted in questionable proceedings, her sentence was never carried out.

SELECTED LANDMARKS: Susan B. Anthony House, Rochester, N.Y. (home); Portrait Monument, U.S. Capitol Rotunda, Washington, D.C.; Mount Hope Cemetery, Rochester, N.Y. (gravesite)

QUOTABLE WORDS: "No matter what is done or is not done, how you are criticized or misunderstood, or what efforts are made to block your path, remember that the only fear you need have is the fear of not standing by the thing you believe to be right." –March, 1906, advice to Anna Howard Shaw

ALICE STONE BLACKWELL

BORN: Sept. 14, 1857, Orange, N.J. ◦— **DIED:** March 15, 1950, Cambridge, Mass., age 92

BACKGROUND: Alice Stone Blackwell, the only child of Lucy Stone and Henry Browne Blackwell, grew up witnessing the formative years of the woman suffrage movement. After earning one of the early degrees granted to women by Boston University, she joined her mother on the suffrage front lines at the American Woman Suffrage Association and edited its *Woman's Journal.* She never married.

CONTRIBUTION TO WOMAN SUFFRAGE: Alice Stone Blackwell helped negotiate the merger of the American and National Woman Suffrage Associations and served as an officer of the united organization for nearly 20 years. Blackwell edited the weekly *Woman's Journal* for more than three decades, making it a must-read for any serious suffragist. Susan B. Anthony even subscribed to it during her years of involvement with the rival National Woman Suffrage Association. Blackwell retired as editor in 1917.

SELECTED LANDMARKS: Forest Hills Cemetery, Jamaica Plain, Mass. (gravesite)

QUOTABLE WORDS: "Great wrongs still remain. . . . The lives of the old worthies are a bugle call to the new generation to take up the fight against them."–1930, from *Lucy Stone*

HARRIOT STANTON BLATCH

BORN: Jan. 20, 1856, Seneca Falls, N.Y. ∽ DIED: Nov. 20, 1940, Greenwich, Conn., age 84

BACKGROUND: Harriot Stanton Blatch was born in Seneca Falls seven and a half years after the famous convention organized by her mother, Elizabeth Cady Stanton. She grew up, quite literally, with the woman suffrage movement. After gaining a bachelor's and a master's degree from Vassar College, she lived in England for 20 years with her British husband.

CONTRIBUTION TO WOMAN SUFFRAGE: Harriot Stanton Blatch recognized that the growing number of women trade workers made ideal supporters for woman suffrage. She worked to interest them in the cause, using skills acquired during years of reform work in England. The versatile Blatch was just as capable of hiking the length of Manhattan door to door in a blizzard to recruit participants for a rally as she was of calling on the President of the United States with a plea for voting rights. She was so determined to vote in 1916 that she established an address in Kansas (after it became a suffrage state) so she could vote there.

SELECTED LANDMARKS: Women's Rights National Historical Park (birthplace), Seneca Falls, N.Y.; Woodlawn Cemetery, Bronx, N.Y. (gravesite)

QUOTABLE WORDS: "We've got to bring to the President, individually, day by day, week in and week out, the idea that great numbers of women want to be free, *will* be free, and want to know what he is going to do about it."–January 9, 1917, as women began picketing against Woodrow Wilson at the White House

LUCY BURNS

BORN: July 28, 1879, Brooklyn, N.Y. ∽ DIED: Dec. 22, 1966, Brooklyn, N.Y., age 87

BACKGROUND: Lucy Burns graduated from Vassar College in 1902 and went on to study linguistics at Yale University and abroad. She set aside studies at Oxford University in order to participate in the radical British suffrage movement of the early 20th century.

CONTRIBUTION TO WOMAN SUFFRAGE: Lucy Burns drew on her experiences in Britain (where she earned a medal for bravery) during frontline service with the U.S. fight for women's voting rights. Alice Paul credited Burns with being "extremely courageous, a thousand times more courageous than I was." Burns implemented many of Paul's most militant protest plans. Her example helped inspire others to practice civil disobedience in order to gain their suffrage rights. She worked behind the scenes, as well, with the editing of the group's newsletter, *The Suffragist*.

SELECTED LANDMARKS: Sewall-Belmont House (National Woman's Party headquarters and museum), Washington, D.C.

QUOTABLE WORDS: "It is unthinkable that a national government which represents women, and which appeals periodically for the suffrages of women, should ignore the issue of the right of all women to political freedom."–December, 1913, address to the annual convention of NAWSA

CARRIE CHAPMAN CATT

BORN: Jan. 9, 1859, Ripon, Wis. ∽ DIED: March 9, 1947, New Rochelle, N.Y., age 88

BACKGROUND: Carrie Clinton Lane was born, raised, and educated in the Midwest, having graduated from Iowa State College in 1880. She was a delegate from Iowa at the first convention of the newly merged NAWSA. She consulted with Lucy Stone and collaborated with Susan B. Anthony. Her interest in suffrage was so keen that, before her second marriage in 1890, she signed a legal agreement with her fiancé granting her four months a year for suffrage work.

CONTRIBUTION TO WOMAN SUFFRAGE: When Susan B. Anthony retired from NAWSA in 1900, she chose Carrie Chapman Catt to take her place. Family illness forced Catt to resign four years later, but she continued to support the cause when she could, both in the U.S. and abroad. In 1916 Catt agreed reluctantly to resume leadership of NAWSA. Then, it is told, she "wept as she had never wept before," knowing how difficult the job would be. Her tireless guidance helped assure the passage and ratification of the 19th Amendment.

SELECTED LANDMARKS: Charles City, Iowa (home); Woodlawn Cemetery, Bronx, N.Y. (gravesite)

QUOTABLE WORDS: "Roll up your sleeves, set your mind to making history and wage such a fight for liberty that the whole world will respect our sex."–November 1915, calling women to try again for woman suffrage in New York State following a recent referendum defeat

INEZ MILHOLLAND

BORN: Aug. 6, 1886, Brooklyn, N.Y. ∽ DIED: Nov. 25, 1916, Los Angeles, Calif., age 30

BACKGROUND: Inez Milholland took up the cause of woman suffrage during her student days at Vassar College, and is said to have recruited more than half of her classmates to support the cause. When the college president refused to let visiting suffrage leaders speak to students on campus, Milholland organized a secret off-campus meeting at a nearby cemetery. She went on to earn a law degree from New York University and marry a European businessman. (Sometimes she is referred to by her married name of Boissevain.)

CONTRIBUTION TO WOMAN SUFFRAGE: Milholland practiced law in New York City, defending the rights of laborers and helping women with divorce proceedings. She led New York's 1912 suffrage parade, on horseback, the year before serving as the horse-riding herald for the march through the nation's capital. Milholland's health was weakened by pernicious anemia, a chronic blood disorder, when she undertook the western speaking tour that claimed her life. Thousands of supporters mourned her death with a Christmas Day memorial service under the dome of the U.S. Capitol. She was the first woman to receive this honor.

SELECTED LANDMARKS: Sewall-Belmont House (National Woman's Party headquarters and museum), Washington, D.C.

QUOTABLE WORDS: "Together we shall stand shoulder to shoulder for the greatest principle the world has ever known, the right of self-government."–Fall 1916, "Party in Power" speech

LUCRETIA MOTT

BORN: Jan. 3, 1793, Nantucket, Mass. — DIED: Nov. 11, 1880, near Philadelphia, Penn., age 87

BACKGROUND: Lucretia Coffin married James Mott when she was 18. Her husband shared her lifelong devotion to reforming their Quaker faith, ending slavery, and expanding the rights of women. The severe style of Mott's Quaker clothing failed to conceal her liveliness or the spark of her witty tongue.

CONTRIBUTION TO WOMAN SUFFRAGE: Lucretia Mott met Elizabeth Cady Stanton in 1840 during London's World Anti-Slavery Convention. After women were banned from speaking at the meeting, Mott and Stanton conferred on the need for women's rights. Their discussions helped spark, eight years later, the convention on that topic at Seneca Falls, New York. Mott continued to influence the movement for women's rights, and its quest for suffrage, for the rest of her life.

SELECTED LANDMARKS: Ship's Inn, Nantucket, Mass. (childhood home); Portrait Monument, U.S. Capitol Rotunda, Washington, D.C.; Fair Hill Burial Ground, Philadelphia, Penn. (gravesite)

QUOTABLE WORDS: "[Woman] is seeking not to be governed by laws in the making of which she has no voice." –December 17, 1849, "Discourse on Woman" speech

ALICE PAUL

BORN: Jan. 11, 1885, Moorestown, N.J. — DIED: July 9, 1977, Moorestown, N.J., age 92

BACKGROUND: Alice Paul never married; she devoted her life to gaining equal rights for women. Her commitment to the campaign for woman suffrage was so complete that she slept in a cold bedroom so she wouldn't stay up reading in bed. (After the 19th Amendment passed Congress, she indulged in detective stories.) Paul worked from an office decorated in suffrage colors with purple velvet upholstery and gold-trimmed walls.

CONTRIBUTION TO WOMAN SUFFRAGE: Alice Paul's militant campaign for women's voting rights helped prod reluctant politicians to take action on the federal suffrage amendment. Harriot Stanton Blatch later asserted: "I am perfectly certain that if it had not been for the National Woman's Party we would not have had national suffrage in the U.S. for another 50 years." Paul assumed everyone shared her enthusiasm for suffrage. During the protests of 1917-19 busy friends and neighbors learned to avoid the area near her National Woman's Party headquarters. Otherwise inevitably she would persuade them—and even passing strangers—to hold a picket banner for a while. "It was impossible to say no to Alice Paul," observed party member Inez Haynes Irwin.

SELECTED LANDMARKS: Paulsdale, Mount Laurel, N.J. (birthplace and retreat); Sewall-Belmont House (National Woman's Party headquarters and museum and her adult home), Washington, D.C.; Westfield Friends Cemetery, Cinnaminson, N.J.(gravesite)

QUOTABLE WORDS: "It is better, as far as getting the vote is concerned I believe, to have a small, united group than an immense debating society."—March 6, 1914, correspondence

ANNA HOWARD SHAW

BORN: Feb. 14, 1847, Newcastle-on-Tyne, England   **DIED**: July 2, 1919, Moylan, Penn., age 72

BACKGROUND: Anna Howard Shaw immigrated to the U.S. with her family at age 4 and grew up on a frontier claim in Michigan. Although she was educated at Boston University as a minister and then as a doctor, the woman suffrage movement increasingly became her work. By her 40th birthday she had taken up the lecture circuit full time for that cause. She never married.

CONTRIBUTION TO WOMAN SUFFRAGE: Because of her ties to both the National and American woman suffrage associations and her friendship with Susan B. Anthony, Anna Howard Shaw became vice president when the two groups merged in 1890. She was passed over as president in 1900 (Carrie Chapman Catt was chosen instead), but she herself became president four years later when Catt unexpectedly resigned. Shaw's strengths as a public speaker far outweighed her skills for management, and she stepped down from the presidency of NAWSA in 1916. She continued to speak in support of suffrage until her death.

SELECTED LANDMARKS: Ashton, Michigan (monument); Big Rapids, Michigan (sculpture and marker)

QUOTABLE WORDS: "As suffragists we have but one belief. . .and that is the right of a human being to have a voice in the government under which he or she lives."–June 21, 1915

ELIZABETH CADY STANTON

BORN: Nov. 12, 1815, Johnstown, N.Y.   **DIED**: Oct. 26, 1902, New York, N.Y., age 86

BACKGROUND: Elizabeth Cady grew up hearing women appeal to her father, an attorney, for help with unjust laws. The young girl tired so of his inability to help that she tried to fix the problem by cutting the "bad laws" out of his law books with scissors. She married Henry Stanton in 1840 at age 24 intent on collaborating with his efforts to abolish slavery. Increased awareness of injustice toward women diverted her to the cause of equal rights. The accompanying photo, taken the year of the women's rights convention at Seneca Falls, shows Stanton with her two oldest sons.

CONTRIBUTION TO WOMAN SUFFRAGE: Elizabeth Cady Stanton devoted most of her adult life to securing women the right to vote. She toured the lecture circuit, wrote extensively on the subject, and lobbied legislators for new laws enfranchising women. In 1866 Stanton became the first woman to seek election to the U.S. House of Representatives. She lost. She is credited with writing the 19th Amendment text.

SELECTED LANDMARKS: Women's Rights National Historical Park, Seneca Falls, N.Y. (including adult residence); Portrait Monument, U.S. Capitol Rotunda, Washington, D.C.; Woodlawn Cemetery, Bronx, N.Y. (gravesite)

QUOTABLE WORDS: "Woman herself must do this work–for woman alone can understand the height, and the depth, the length and the breadth of her own degradation and woe."–August 2, 1848, Second Woman's Rights Convention, Rochester, N.Y.

LUCY STONE

BORN: Aug. 13, 1818 near West Brookfield, Mass. ∽ DIED: Oct. 18, 1893, Dorchester, Mass., age 75

BACKGROUND: When Lucy Stone was born, her mother commented, "Oh dear! I am sorry it is a girl. A woman's life is so hard." Lucy became the first woman from Massachusetts (and one of the first in the nation) to graduate from college (Oberlin College) in 1847. Afterward Stone was so outspoken about women's rights that a popular song called for a man "who with a wedding kiss shuts up the mouth of Lucy Stone." When she married Henry Blackwell at age 36, her wedding vows were rewritten so he could not require her to obey him. She kept her maiden name, too.

CONTRIBUTION TO WOMAN SUFFRAGE: By the time of the Seneca Falls convention on women's rights in 1848 Lucy Stone was already a well-known speaker on the topic; she was hissed at, peppered with eggs, soaked with a fire hose, and mobbed. Stone persevered, often winning over skeptical crowds with her persuasive, melodious voice. Stone protested her "taxation without representation" on many occasions; in 1858 she watched authorities auction off her household goods to recoup unpaid taxes. Stone helped fuel many referenda campaigns and constructed a nationwide organization devoted to woman suffrage.

SELECTED LANDMARKS: West Brookfield, Mass. (birthplace site); Forest Hills Cemetery, Jamaica Plain, Mass. (gravesite)

QUOTABLE WORDS: "If the law can meddle with the woman, why should not the woman meddle with the law?"—childhood query to her mother

SOJOURNER TRUTH

BORN: 1797 (estimated) in Ulster County, N.Y. ∽
DIED: November 26, 1883, Battle Creek, Mich., age about 86

BACKGROUND: Isabella Baumfree was born into slavery and remained the property of others until about the age of 30 when New York State banned the practice. She renamed herself Sojourner Truth in 1843 after feeling commanded by God to speak out against injustice. She found many causes worthy of her efforts—from the faults of slavery to the care of the poor to the need for women's rights.

CONTRIBUTION TO WOMAN SUFFRAGE: Truth's willingness to speak in public at a time when women rarely did so inspired many others to have the courage to voice their beliefs. Her famous "Ain't I a woman" speech took place at one of the early meetings about women's rights. Years later she was reportedly among the women who tried to vote in the presidential election of 1872. Her desire to "sojourn once to the ballot box before I die" never came to pass.

SELECTED LANDMARKS: Oak Hill Cemetery, Battle Creek, Mich. (gravesite)

QUOTABLE WORDS: "If Eve, the first woman God ever made, was strong enough to turn the world upside down all alone, these women together ought to be able to turn it back and get it right side again. And now [that] they are asking to do it, the men better let them!"—conclusion to the "Ain't I a woman" speech, May 29, 1851, Woman's Rights Convention in Akron, Ohio

1788 _____
The U.S. Constitution is adopted to establish a federal government for the United States.

1791 _____
The Bill of Rights is added to the Constitution, but no mention is made of the "right to vote."

1807 _____
New Jersey revokes the right of women to vote in that state, thus ending the only significant access of women to the polls in the nation.

1840 _____
Elizabeth Cady Stanton meets Lucretia Mott during the World Anti-Slavery Convention in London.

1848 _____
The nation's first Woman's Rights Convention is held at Seneca Falls, N.Y., on July 19–20.

Second Woman's Rights Convention is held in Rochester, N.Y., on August 2.

1850 _____
At the April Woman's Rights Convention in Salem, Ohio, men are forbidden to talk.

1851 _____
Elizabeth Cady Stanton meets Susan B. Anthony in March.

1852 _____
Lucy Stone meets Elizabeth Cady Stanton and Susan B. Anthony in May.

1861 _____
Civil War begins on April 12 at Fort Sumter, S.C.

1865 _____
Civil War ends on April 9 at Appomattox Court House, Va.

13th Amendment abolishes slavery.

1866 _____
Elizabeth Cady Stanton is the first woman to run for Congress; she earns 24 votes.

1867 _____
State suffrage is defeated in Kansas and New York.

1868 _____
14th Amendment guarantees black males equal protection under the law. It also defines citizenship and implies that only men can vote.

1869 _____
Wyoming Territory is established with equal suffrage for men and women.

An amendment in favor of woman suffrage is introduced for the first time to the U.S. Congress but never acted upon.

National Woman Suffrage Association (NWSA) is founded in May by Elizabeth Cady Stanton and Susan B. Anthony.

American Woman Suffrage Association (AWSA) is founded in November by Lucy Stone.

1870 _____
15th Amendment guarantees voting rights to all males.

Utah Territory adopts woman suffrage.

1872 _____
Susan B. Anthony is arrested for attempting to vote in Rochester, N.Y.

1874 _____
State suffrage is defeated in Michigan.

1875 _____
U.S. Supreme Court rejects the claim in _Minor v. Happersett_ that women, as citizens, already have the right to vote.

1877 _____
State suffrage is defeated in Colorado.

1878 _____
The final text of the woman suffrage amendment (later called the Susan B. Anthony amendment) is introduced for the first time in the U.S. Congress.

1882

State suffrage is defeated in Nebraska.

1883

Washington Territory adopts woman suffrage.

1884

State suffrage is defeated in Oregon.

1887

State suffrage is defeated in Rhode Island.

Montana Territory adopts woman suffrage.

U.S. Congress abolishes woman suffrage in Utah Territory.

Washington Territorial Supreme Court overturns woman suffrage.

U.S. Senate votes for the first time on the woman suffrage amendment and rejects it 34 to 16 on January 25.

1889

State suffrage is defeated in Washington State.

1890

State suffrage is defeated in South Dakota.

National American Woman Suffrage Association (NAWSA) forms on February 18 with a merger of the National Woman Suffrage Association (NWSA) and the American Woman Suffrage Association (AWSA).

Wyoming becomes the first state to grant women the right to vote. On July 23 it enters the Union and continues the full suffrage it granted as a territory.

1893

Colorado grants women full suffrage rights on its second try.

1894

State suffrage is defeated in Kansas for the second time.

1896

State suffrage is defeated in California.

Idaho and Utah grant women full suffrage rights.

1900

State suffrage is defeated in Oregon for the second time.

1902

State suffrage is defeated in New Hampshire.

1906

State suffrage is defeated in Oregon for the third time.

1908

State suffrage is defeated in Oregon for the fourth time.

1910

First woman suffrage parade occurs in New York City.

Alice Paul meets Lucy Burns at a London police station after the two women are arrested for suffrage militance.

State suffrage is defeated in Oregon for the fifth time and in Oklahoma.

Washington State grants women full suffrage rights on its second try.

1911

National Association Opposed to Woman Suffrage is founded.

California grants women full suffrage rights on its second try.

1912

State suffrage is defeated in Michigan for the second time and in Ohio and Wisconsin.

Arizona grants women full suffrage rights, as does Kansas on its third try, and Oregon on its sixth try.

1913

Alice Paul and Lucy Burns stage the first woman suffrage parade in Washington, D.C., on March 3.

Southern States Woman Suffrage Conference is founded to promote state, not federal, suffrage in the South.

State suffrage is defeated in Michigan for the third time.

Territory of Alaska adopts woman suffrage.

1914

U.S. Senate votes for the second time on the woman suffrage amendment and rejects it 35 to 34 on March 19.

NAWSA forces Alice Paul and her radical suffrage activities out of its organization.

State suffrage is defeated in Nebraska, Ohio, and South Dakota for the second time and in Missouri and North Dakota.

Montana and Nevada grant women full suffrage rights.

1915

U.S. House votes for the first time on the woman suffrage amendment and rejects it 204 to 174 on January 12.

New York City stages its largest woman suffrage parade ever with 30,000 or more participants.

State suffrage is defeated in New York for the second time and in Massachusetts, New Jersey, and Pennsylvania.

1916

Carrie Chapman Catt proposes her Winning Plan during a NAWSA convention in Atlantic City, N.J., in September.

NAWSA establishes Suffrage House in Washington, D.C., to help with lobbying for the federal amendment.

State suffrage is defeated in Iowa and West Virginia.

Jeannette Rankin, representative from Montana, becomes the first woman elected to serve in the U.S. Congress.

Inez Milholland dies on November 25 and is memorialized on December 25 in a service at the U.S. Capitol.

1917

Women begin picketing on January 10 in front of the White House with demands for suffrage.

National Woman's Party is formed in early March; 1,000 members, in an effort to meet with the President, march around the White House.

Anthony amendment is introduced for consideration in the U.S. House and Senate on April 2 and 4, respectively.

U.S. declares war on Germany on April 6.

National Woman's Party posts "Russian Banners" at the White House on June 20.

First National Woman's Party pickets are arrested June 22 and sentenced to jail June 26.

National Woman's Party posts "Kaiser Banner" at the White House on August 14.

Alice Paul is arrested on October 20 and jailed soon after for picketing the White House; she begins her hunger strike and is committed to the psychiatric ward.

Suffragists are subjected to "Night of Terror" upon arrival at Occoquan Workhouse on November 15; judge rules their detention illegal November 23.

National Woman's Party jailbirds are awarded prison pins on December 6.

State suffrage is defeated in Maine.

New York grants women full suffrage rights on its third try.

1918

U.S. House votes for the second time on the woman suffrage amendment and passes it for the first time, 274 to 136, on January 10.

National Woman's Party revives protests with demonstrations in Lafayette Square on August 6.

U.S. Senate votes for the third time on the woman suffrage amendment and it falls short of passage by two votes, 62 to 34, on October 1.

A truce ends the fighting of World War I on November 11.

State suffrage is defeated in Louisiana.

Michigan on its fourth try, Oklahoma on its second try, and South Dakota on its third try, grant women full suffrage.

1919

National Woman's Party establishes a watch fire in front of the White House on January 1.

U.S. Senate votes for the fourth time on the woman suffrage amendment and it falls short of passage by one vote, 63 to 33, on February 10.

U.S. House votes for the third time on the woman suffrage amendment and passes it for the second time, 304 to 89 on May 21.

U.S. Senate votes for the fifth time on the woman suffrage amendment and passes it 66 to 30 on June 4.

Wisconsin becomes the first state to ratify the 19th Amendment on June 10.

1920

Tennessee secures ratification of the 19th Amendment on August 18 as the 36th state to approve it.

U.S. secretary of state declares the 19th Amendment ratified on August 26.

★ RESOURCE GUIDE

BOOKS FOR YOUNG READERS

Bolden, Tonya (editor). *33 things every girl should know about women's history, from suffragettes to skirt lengths to the E.R.A.* New York: Crown Publishers, 2002.

Fritz, Jean. *You Want Women to Vote, Lizzie Stanton?* New York: G.P. Putnam's Sons, 1995.

Guernsey, JoAnn Bren. *Voices of Feminism: Past, Present, and Future.* Minneapolis: Lerner, 1996.

Harness, Cheryl. *Remember the Ladies: 100 Great American Women.* New York: HarperCollins, 2001.

Helmer, Diana Star. *Women Suffragists.* New York: Facts on File, Inc., 1998.

Lasky, Kathyrn. *Dear America: A Time for Courage—The Suffragette Diary of Kathleen Bowen, Washington, D.C., 1917* (fictionalized). New York: Scholastic, 2001.

VIDEOS

"Iron Jawed Angels," dramatization about Alice Paul and the National Woman's Party directed by Katja Von Garnier. HBO films, 2004. www.iron-jawed-angels.com/

"Not for Ourselves Alone: The Story of Elizabeth Cady Stanton and Susan B. Anthony," documentary film by Ken Burns and Paul Barnes. Public Broadcasting Service, 1999.

"One Woman, One Vote," *The American Experience,* Public Broadcasting Service. Educational Film Center, 1996. www.pbs.org/onewoman/one_woman.html

PLACES TO VISIT

"From Parlor to Politics: Women and Reform in America, 1890-1925," permanent exhibit at the National Museum of American History, Smithsonian Institution, Washington, D.C.

Sewall-Belmont House and Museum, National Woman's Party headquarters, Washington, D.C. www.sewallbelmont.org

The Women's Museum, Dallas, Texas. www.thewomensmuseum.org/

Women's Rights National Historical Park, Seneca Falls, N.Y. www.nps.gov/wori/wrnhp.htm

WEB SITES

Alice Paul Institute www.alicepaul.org

"Declaration of Rights and Sentiments" text www.search.eb.com/women/pri/Q00172.html

Encyclopedia Britannica, "Women in American History" www.search.eb.com/women/

www.equalrightsamendment.org

League of Women Voters www.lwv.org/

Library of Congress, "National American Woman Suffrage Association Collection" lcweb2.loc.gov/ammem/naw/nawshome.html

The National Women's Hall of Fame www.greatwomen.org/home.php

Women of the West museum www.autry-museum.org/explorc/exhibits/suffrage/index.html

Memories of my childhood meeting with Alice Paul were rekindled by Joan Hoff's profile of her in *Forgotten Heroes*. Thus began the research for this book. I started my exploration with *Century of Struggle* by Eleanor Flexner. This comprehensive history of women's rights in the United States is as informative and readable today as it was when it was first published in 1959. Alexander Keyssar's *The Right to Vote* helped me understand the larger context of voting rights in the United States.

I supplemented my reading with visits to several key sites from woman suffrage history, starting with the Women's Rights National Historical Park in Seneca Falls, N.Y. Places visited during two research trips to Washington, D.C., included the Sewall-Belmont House and Museum (headquarters for the National Woman's Party), the National Archives, the Smithsonian Institution, and the Library of Congress.

Edward James's massive anthology of biographical sketches, *Notable American Women*, provided important general background on suffragists. So did a number of biographies. Sources of particular interest are noted below along with citations for quoted text. Citation abbreviations are spelled out when first introduced. A bibliography of all consulted works follows these entries.

CHAPTER 1 ★ PARADE, 1913 _____

Two suffragists—Doris Stevens and Inez Haynes Irwin—recorded eyewitness accounts of Alice Paul's suffrage activities. I consulted their works—*Jailed for Freedom* and *The Story of Alice Paul,* respectively—for this chapter and others dealing with the subject of suffrage militancy. Linda Ford's contemporary study of the topic, *Iron-Jawed Angels,* was an invaluable resource. I gathered further details about the 1913 parade from period newspaper accounts, transcripts from Senate hearings that investigated parade activities, and surviving photographs of the event in collections at the Library of Congress and the archives of the National Woman's Party.

CITATIONS. *Raised quotes:* p. 15 (*New York Times*, March 5, 1913:8). *Text:* p. 12, Great Demand Banner (Irwin: 30); p. 15, police officer: ". . . if you women would all stay at home." (U.S. Senate Committee: 70); p. 15, woman participant: "would have taken better care..." (*New York Times*, March 5, 1913:8); p. 15, Anna Howard Shaw (AHS): "There seemed to be a tacit agreement . . ." (*New York Times*, March 5, 1913:8).

CHAPTER 2 ★ RIGHTS, 1848–1906 _____

Flexner's *Century of Struggle* provides an indispensable overview of the period summarized here. Helpful biographies of central figures were Elizabeth Griffith's vivid picture of Elizabeth Cady Stanton, *In Her Own Right;* Margaret Hope Bacon's *Valiant Friend: The Life of Lucretia Mott;* Andrea Moore Kerr's *Lucy Stone: Speaking Out for Equality;* and Kathleen Barry's *Susan B. Anthony.*

Other sources that helped identify the personalities and complexities of 19th-century reform efforts included Judith E. Harper's *Susan B. Anthony: A Biographical Companion,* Barbara Goldsmith's *Other Powers: The Age of Suffrage, Spiritualism, and the Scandalous Victoria Woodhull,* and Linda Kerber's essay "Women and the Constitution" in Marjorie Spruill Wheeler's *One Woman, One Vote.* The latter provided background on early voting rights for women. Alan Grimes's study of *The Puritan Ethic and Woman Suffrage* suggests the motivation for granting woman suffrage in the West. Rosalyn Terborg-Penn offers scholarship about diversity among suffragists through works like *African American Women in the Struggle for the Vote*. Marjorie Spruill Wheeler traces the regional evolution of the cause with *New Women of the New South*.

CITATIONS. *Raised quotes:* p. 18 (Griffith: 164-65); p. 19 (Stanton, *History of Woman Suffrage, Vol. I: 629-30*); p. 22 (Frost and Cullen-DuPont: 399). *Photo captions:* p. 17, George H. Williams of Oregon: "make every home a hell on earth." (Flexner: 142); p. 23, Elizabeth Cady Stanton (ECS): "like two sticks of a drum . . ." (Griffith: 182); p. 23, ECS: "You must make the puddings . . ." (Griffith: 97). *Text:* p. 18, ECS: ". . . to do and dare anything." (Flexner: 69); p. 18, announcement (Frost and Cullen-DuPont: 85); p. 18, Declaration of Sentiments (Frost and Cullen-DuPont 359-61); p. 18, Lucretia Mott (LM): "make us [look] ridiculous" (Bacon, 1980: 128); p. 19, *Mechanic's Advocate:* July–August, 1848: "would set the world by the ears." (Frost and Cullen-DuPont: 88); p. 19, Frederick Douglass, *The North Star,* July 28, 1848: "a discussion of the rights of animals . . ." (Frost and Cullen-DuPont: 86); pp. 20–21, Sojourner Truth: "Ain't I a woman?" speech (Frost and Cullen-DuPont: 104-05); p. 22, Lucy Stone (LS): ". . . get out of the terrible pit" (Flexner: 138); p. 23, LS: ". . . tell him you want to vote." (Kerr: 158); p. 24, George Vest, Democrat of Missouri: ". . . touch of a true woman" (Flexner: 167); p. 25, Susan B. Anthony (SBA): ". . . failure is impossible!" (Judith Harper: 34).

CHAPTER 3 ★ MOMENTUM, 1906–1916 _____

Midge Mackenzie's *Shoulder to Shoulder* uses eyewitness accounts to chronicle Britain's militant woman suffrage movement. Ford recaps some of this history in *Iron-Jawed Angels,* as do Inez Haynes Irwin and Doris Stevens. I gained additional information by reading newspaper accounts of British suffragette activity as reported in *The New York Times.* Data for the chapter's map is from Alexander Keyssar's *The Right to Vote.*

In addition to Flexner's overview, I relied on several biographies about U.S. suffragists from the turn of the century. These include Ellen Carol DuBois's book *Harriot Stanton Blatch and the Winning of Woman Suffrage,* the works about Paul by Stevens and Irwin, and *Carrie Chapman Catt: A Public Life* by Jacqueline Van Voris. Several essays in Marjorie Wheeler's *One Woman, One Vote* were helpful, including Ellen Carol DuBois's study of Blatch, the Robert Booth Fowler commentary on Catt, and Manuela Thurner's essay on antisuffragists.

CITATIONS. *Raised quotes:* p. 29 (Flexner: 229); p. 33 (Van Voris: 121); p. 35 (Ford: 71). *Photo captions:* p. 28, Harriot Stanton Blatch (HSB): ". . . trying to push an unpopular cause." (DuBois, *HSB*: 105). *Text:* p. 28, HSB: "There did not seem to be . . ." (Flexner: 242); p. 28, Inez Haines: ". . . it is actually fashionable now." (DuBois, *HSB*: 109); p. 28, Rheta Childe Dorr: "suffrage was a thing . . . to die for." (Ford: 33); p. 32, mutual friend: ". . .one spirit and one brain." (Irwin: 18); p. 35, Carrie Chapman Catt (CCC): "red-hot, never-ceasing campaign." (Van Voris: 135); p. 35, CCC: "those who enter on this task . . ." (Flexner: 273); p. 35, CCC: "keep so much 'suffrage noise' going . . ." (Flexner: 273-74); p. 35, Woodrow Wilson (WW): "you can afford a little while to wait." (Ford: 73); p. 35, AHS: "We have waited so long . . ." (Flexner: 272); p. 36, Miriam F. Leslie: "the cause of woman suffrage." (Flexner: 265); p. 36, Maud Wood Park: "For the first time our goal looked possible . . ." (Van Voris: 135); p. 36: Inez Milholland (IM): ". . . how long must this go on . . ." (Ford: 75); p. 37, HSB: ". . .We have to take a new departure." (Stevens; 57).

CHAPTER 4 ★ PROTEST, 1917 _____

Ford offers the best contemporary examination of militant suffragists and of the reactions they provoked in *Iron-Jawed Angels.* I extended my understanding of the period using two of her primary sources, the previously cited works by Irwin and Stevens. Both authors present dramatic eyewitness accounts of demonstrations and mob violence, such as the events that unfolded with the "Kaiser Banner." Judith Stiehm's *Nonviolent Power* places suffrage civil disobedience within a broader historical context.

CITATIONS. *Raised quotes:* p. 40 (Ford: 189); p. 47 (Irwin: 252). *Text:* p. 39, banners (Stevens: 59); p. 39, Alice Paul (AP): "Our banners were really beautiful." (Ford: 126); p. 40 Doris Stevens (DS): "When *will* that woman come . . ." (Ford:127); p. 41, DS: "as if the long line of purple . . ." (Stevens: 66) [DS also notes: "This one single incident probably did more than any other to make women sacrifice themselves," (Ford: 133-34)]; p. 41, WW: "We shall fight . . ." (Ferrell: 3); p. 41, votes-for-women-first policy (Irwin: 207); p. 42: DS: "The inconsistency between . . ." (Stevens: 69); p. 42, descriptors of pickets (Stevens: 59 and Ford: 151); p. 42 exchange between AP and police chief (Stevens: 75); p. 43, Inez Haynes Irwin (IHI): "the slow growth of the crowds . . ." (Irwin: 488); p. 46, banner (Ford: 158); page 46, Anne Martin: "So long as you send women to jail . . ." (Irwin: 479); p. 47, AP letter to her mother (Ford: 176); p. 47, Ada Davenport Kendall in the *Buffalo Express,* September 1917: (Ford: 160).

CHAPTER 5 ★ PRISON, 1917

The trio of books about the National Woman's Party by Ford, Stevens, and Irwin provide considerable detail about the treatment of jailed suffragists. *The Story of Alice Paul* proved particularly helpful with its lengthy quoting from eyewitnesses. As elsewhere, Flexner summarizes the same history briefly in *Century of Struggle*.

CITATIONS. *Raised quotes:* p. 51 (Ford: 208); p. 54 (Stevens: 122); p. 55 (Ford: 182). *Photo captions:* p. 50, boy: "Three months you'll be waiting." (Irwin: 483); p. 59, Alva Belmont: "A flame of rebellion . . ." (Stevens: 132). *Text:* p. 49, AHS: "No one can feel worse . . ." (Ford: 128); p. 49, CCC: "unwise and unprofitable to the cause." (Van Voris: 145); p. 49 NAWSA wartime policy (Van Voris: 138); p. 51, mother of Natalie Gray, the daughter sent "to fight for democracy at home." (Ford: 159-160); p. 51, suffrage husband: "It's got to be love at first sight . . ." (Ford: 211); p. 51, suffrage husband who could "get along" (Ford: 214); p. 54, suffrage song: "We worried Woody Wood as we stood . . ." (Ford: 277-78); p. 55, AP: "I am being imprisoned . . ." (Irwin: 292); p. 55, AP: "However gaily you start out in prison . . ." (Stevens: 114); p. 57, Elizabeth McShane's description of force-feeding (Ford: 181-82); p. 58, DS text: "slender file of women . . ." (Stevens: 129).

CHAPTER 6 ★ ACTION, 1918–1919

Although Flexner provides an overview of the final ratification struggle in *Century of Struggle*, I relied more on the books by Stevens, Irwin, Ford, and Van Voris when presenting my summary. The latter adds the perspective of NAWSA activities in balance to the National Woman's Party efforts portrayed in the former three works. Two volumes from a series on *The Wilson Era* by Josephus Daniels, a member of the President's administration, add insight about Wilson's attitude and effort toward woman suffrage during the period. Robert Ferrell's work, *Woodrow Wilson and World War I* helped as well.

CITATIONS. *Raised quotes:* p. 63 (Van Voris: 149); p. 64 (Irwin: 367); p. 67 (Irwin: 333); p. 69 (Flexner: 165). *Photo captions:* p. 65, Pauline Adams: "some say we ought to be *tarred and feathered."* (Ford: 187-88); p. 66, IHI: "Everything and everybody smelled of kerosene." (Irwin: 484). *Text:* p. 61, comments of legislators (Stevens: 135); p. 63, unnamed suffragist: "That sense we had of her . . ." (Irwin: 335); p. 64, Mary Winsor: "It is quite enough . . ." (Irwin: 368); p. 64, WW: "urge the passage . . ." (Stevens: 146); p. 64, Lucy Branham: "The torch which I hold . . ." (Stevens: 147); p. 64, WW: "Shall we admit them only . . ." (Flexner: 302-03); p. 65, James Reed: "There are some differences . . ." (Ford: 231); p. 66, Olympia Brown: "I have fought for liberty . . ." (Stevens: 159); p. 67, DS: "as fast as he made them . . ." (Stevens: 161); p. 67, IHI: "ran about in hordes." (Irwin: 418); p. 67, John Sharp Williams, Democrat of Mississippi: "stopped making fools of themselves." (Ferrell: 210); pp. 68-69, DS: "two hundred policemen in close formation rushed us . . ." [DS adds: "Women were knocked down and trampled under foot, some of them almost unconscious, others bleeding from the hands and face; arms were bruised and twisted; pocket-books were snatched and wrist-watches stolen."] (Stevens: 177-79)

CHAPTER 7 ★ VICTORY, 1919–1920

Irwin's comprehensive summary of ratification votes in *The Story of Alice Paul* proved most helpful in understanding the ratification timetable as shared in the text and chapter map. I referred to Alexander Keyssar's *The Right to Vote* for additional background. Also useful were the Van Voris biography on *Carrie Chapman Catt* and Flexner's history. Anastatia Sim's essay, "Armageddon in Tennessee: The Final Battle Over the Nineteenth Amendment," from *One Woman, One Vote* brought that struggle to life.

CITATIONS. *Raised quotes:* p. 73, letter to Marjorie Shuler: (Flexner: 310); p. 76 (Irwin: 464); p. 79, address to the Tennessee legislature explaining his vote: (Frost and Cullen-DuPont: 335); p. 81 (Ford: 246). *Photo captions:* p. 77, Confederate veteran: "'fought and bled' for Tennessee . . ." (from original caption supplied by Tennessee State Library and Archives, Josephine Pearson papers). *Text:* p. 73, CCC letter to Marjorie Shuler, July 1, 1919: ". . . with your shield or upon it." (Flexner: 310); p. 76, CCC letter to Mary Peck, Aug. 15, 1920: "We now have . . ." (Van Voris: 159); p. 76, telegram signed by 63 antisuffrage legislators from North Carolina: "to the last ditch . . ." (Sims in Wheeler: 334); p. 78, CCC, *Woman Citizen*, Sept. 4, 1920: "Never in the history of politics . . ." (Van Voris: 160); p. 79, CCC letter to Mary Peck, Aug. 15, 1920: "Even if we win . . ." (Van Voris: 160); p. 79, Febb Burn's letter to her son Harry: "Hurrah! And vote for suffrage . . ." (Frost and Cullen-DuPont: 335); p. 80, Harry Burn, address to the Tennessee legislature explaining his vote: "I knew that a mother's advice . . ." (Frost and Cullen-DuPont: 335).

AFTERWORD

Keyssar's *The Right to Vote* explains the evolving status of voting rights since passage of the 19th Amendment. Rosalyn Terborg-Penn explains the continued voter discrimination against black women after the 19th Amendment in the two works cited about African-American women and suffrage.

The extensive study of *Women and Politics Worldwide,* edited by Barbara J. Nelson and Najma Chowdhury, provided facts on international suffrage for women. Van Voris describes the evolution of NAWSA into today's League of Women Voters in *Carrie Chapman Catt.* Biographical essays in the James study of *Notable American Women* provided details about the fate of some key suffragists. For Alice Paul I relied on the Hoff essay from *Forgotten Heroes* as well as the books by Ford and Stevens (including the helpful introduction by Edith Mayo in the latter). Hoff explains the history of the equal rights amendment in her essay.

CITATIONS. *Raised quotes:* p. 85 (Ford in Wheeler: 293). *Text:* p. 88, DS: "When all suffrage controversy has died away . . ." (Stevens: 183); p. 89, CCC: "This is a glorious . . . day . . ." (Van Voris: 162).

PROFILES & OTHER TEXT

I consulted biographies, the James compendium, Harper's *Biographical Companion,* and online and news media sources to prepare profiles of key women suffragists.

CITATIONS. *Raised quote:* p. 9, (Ford:189). *Photo captions:* p. 1 image (caption p. 109); song lyrics: ". . . They will not vote without us." ("Hurrah for Woman Suffrage!" cassette). *Profiles:* p. 92, SBA: "No matter what is done . . ." (Judith Harper: 34); p. 92, Alice Stone Blackwell: "Great wrongs . . ." (Blackwell: 298); p. 93, HSB: "We've got to bring to the President . . ." (DuBois, *HSB:* 202); p. 93, AP: ". . . more courageous than I was." (Ford: 25); p. 93, Lucy Burns: "It is unthinkable . . ." (Stevens, 1920 edition.: 26); p. 94, Gertrude Brown about CCC: "wept as she had never wept before." (Van Voris: 130); p. 94, CCC: "Roll up your sleeves . . ." (Van Voris: 129); p. 94, IM: "Together we shall stand . . ." (Stevens, 1920 edition: 50); p. 95, LM: "[Woman] is seeking . . ." (Bacon, 1999: 153); p. 95, HSB: "I am perfectly certain . . ." (DuBois, *HSB:* 212); p. 95, IHI: "It was impossible . . ." (Irwin: 23); p. 95, AP letter to Eunice R. Oberly: "It is better . . ." (Partnow: 283); p. 96, AHS: "As suffragists we have . . ." (Linkugel: 258-92); p. 96, ECS: "Woman herself . . ." (Griffith: 61); p. 97, mother of Lucy Stone: "Oh dear! I am sorry it is a girl . . ." (Blackwell: 3); p. 97, Boston *Post,* 1855: ". . . shuts up the mouth of Lucy Stone." (Kerr: 85); p. 97, LS: "If the law can meddle . . ." (Kerr: 85); p. 97, Sojourner Truth (ST): "sojourn once to the ballot box . . ." (Sherr: 222); p. 97, ST: ". . . the men better let them!" (Frost and Cullen-DuPont: 105).

ACKNOWLEDGMENTS

Many people deserve recognition for their help in creating this book, beginning with family members whose patience with a preoccupied spouse and mother is most appreciated. I'm grateful to my father for introducing me to Alice Paul, and to my mother, who descends from a courageous stock of women, for teaching me about the importance of cloth.

Special thanks are due to those individuals and institutions that have shared images for publication; they are acknowledged in detail on page 109. It was a pleasure to borrow two images from Coline Jenkins, the fourth-generation female descendant of Elizabeth Cady Stanton. I owe a special debt to Jennifer Spencer and the Sewall-Belmont House museum. Jennifer opened the photo archives of the National Woman's Party for my review not once, but twice, and many images from her remarkable collection strengthen this book. I treasure the afternoon spent thanks to Lisa Kathleen Graddy reviewing suffrage banners in the collection of the Smithsonian's National Museum of American History.

Jennifer Spencer deserves further thanks for reviewing page proofs of the book, as do historians Linda Ford, Elisabeth Griffith, and Edith Mayo. Writing by each of these scholars was helpful to my work, and their willingness to review my own project is much appreciated.

Finally I would like to thank the many women working for the National Geographic Society—beginning with my editor Jennifer Emmett—who nurtured this project from the germ of an idea years ago into a book. Two of these women even brought daughters into the world during our collective labor. Men helped along the way, too (thank you), but it seems especially fitting that so many female hands played a part in bringing this piece of woman's history to life.

"Army Ends Its Hike; General Jones Scores." *The New York Times* (New York), March 1, 1913: 6.

Bacon, Margaret Hope. *Valiant Friend—The Life of Lucretia Mott.* Philadelphia: Friends General Conference, 1980, 1999.

Barnhart, Robert K. (editor). *The Barnhart Dictionary of Etymology.* Bronx, New York: H.W. Wilson Co., 1988.

Barry, Kathleen. *Susan B. Anthony: A Biography of a Singular Feminist.* Bloomington, Indiana: 1st Books Library, 2000.

Bernhard, Virginia, and Elizabeth Fox-Genovese, (editors). *The Birth of American Feminism—The Seneca Falls Convention of 1848.* St. James, New York: Brandywine Press, 1995.

Blackwell, Alice Stone. *Lucy Stone: Pioneer of Woman's Rights.* Norwood, Massachusetts: Plimpton Press, 1930.

Catt, Carrie Chapman, and Nettie Rogers Shuler. *Woman Suffrage and Politics: The Inner Story of the Suffrage Movement.* New York, New York: Charles Scribner's Sons, 1926.

Chambers-Schiller, Lee Virginia. *Liberty, A Better Husband—Single Women in America: The Generations of 1780-1840.* New Haven, Connecticut: Yale University Press, 1984.

Cott, Nancy F. "Across the Great Divide: Women in Politics Before and After 1920." *One Woman, One Vote—Rediscovering the Woman Suffrage Movement,* edited by Marjorie Spruill Wheeler, 353–73. Troutdale, Oregon: NewSage Press, 1995.

____ . "The Great Demand." *Days of Destiny—Crossroads in American History,* edited by James M. McPherson and Alan Brinkley, 248–63. New York: Dorling Kindersley, 2001.

Daniels, Josephus. *The Wilson Era: Years of Peace—1910–1917.* Chapel Hill: The University of North Carolina Press, 1944.

____ . *The Wilson Era: Years of War and After—1917–1923.* Chapel Hill: The University of North Carolina Press, 1946.

DuBois, Ellen Carol (editor). *The Elizabeth Cady Stanton-Susan B. Anthony Reader.* Boston: Northeastern University Press, 1981, 1992.

____ . *Harriot Stanton Blatch and the Winning of Woman Suffrage.* New Haven, Connecticut: Yale University Press, 1997.

Ferrell, Robert H. *Woodrow Wilson and World War 1: 1917–1921.* New York: Harper & Row, 1985.

"5,000 Women March, Beset by Crowds." *The New York Times* (New York), March 4, 1913: 5.

Flexner, Eleanor, and Ellen Fitzpatrick (editor). *Century of Struggle: The Woman's Rights Movement in the United States.* Cambridge, Massachusetts: The Belknap Press of Harvard University Press, 1959, 1975, 1996.

Ford, Linda G. "Alice Paul and the Triumph of Militancy." *One Woman, One Vote—Rediscovering the Woman Suffrage Movement,* edited by Marjorie Spruill Wheeler, 277–294. Troutdale, Oregon: NewSage Press, 1995.

____ . *Iron-Jawed Angels: The Suffrage Militancy of the National Woman's Party, 1912–1920.* Lanham, Maryland: University Press of America, 1991.

Fowler, Robert Booth. *Carrie Catt: Feminist Politician.* Boston: Northeastern University Press, 1986.

____ . "Carrie Chapman Catt, Strategist." *One Woman, One Vote—Rediscovering the Woman Suffrage Movement,* edited by Marjorie Spruill Wheeler, 295–314. Troutdale, Oregon: NewSage Press, 1995.

Frost, Elizabeth, and Kathryn Cullen-DuPont. *Women's Suffrage in America—An Eyewitness History.* New York: Facts On File, 1992.

Gluck, Sherna. *From Parlor to Prison: Five American Suffragists Talk About Their Lives.* New York: Vintage, 1976.

Goldsmith, Barbara. *Other Powers—The Age of Suffrage, Spiritualism, and the Scandalous Victoria Woodhull.* New York: Alfred A. Knopf, 1998.

Griffith, Elisabeth. *In Her Own Right—The Life of Elizabeth Cady Stanton.* New York: Oxford University Press, 1984.

Grimes, Alan P. *The Puritan Ethic and Woman Suffrage.* New York: Oxford University Press, 1967.

Harper, Ida Husted. *The Life and Work of Susan B. Anthony.* Indianapolis, Indiana: The Hollenbeck Press, 1908.

Harper, Judith E. *Susan B. Anthony—A Biographical Companion.* Santa Barbara, California: ABC-CLIO, 1998.

Hoff, Joan. "Alice Paul: Friend and Foe of the Equal Rights Amendment." *Forgotten Heroes,* edited by Susan Ware, 221–30. New York: The Free Press, 1998.

"Hurrah for Woman Suffrage!" (cassette tape with printed lyrics). *Songs from the American Woman Suffrage Movement 1848–1920.* Beverly Hills, California: Miriam Reed Productions, 1995.

Irwin, Inez Haynes. *The Story of Alice Paul and the National Woman's Party.* Fairfax, Virginia: Denlinger's Publishers, 1964, 1977.

James, Edward T. (editor). *Notable American Women.* Cambridge, Massachusetts: The Belknap Press of Harvard University Press, 1971.

Kerber, Linda K. "'Ourselves and Our Daughters Forever': Women and the Constitution, 1787–1876." *One Woman, One Vote—Rediscovering the Woman Suffrage Movement,* edited by Marjorie Spruill Wheeler, 21–36. Troutdale, Oregon: NewSage Press, 1995.

Kerr, Andrea Moore. *Lucy Stone: Speaking Out for Equality.* New Brunswick, New Jersey: Rutgers University Press, 1992.

Keyssar, Alexander. *The Right to Vote—The Contested History of Democracy in the United States.* New York: Basic Books, 2000.

Linkugel, Wilmer A. "The Speeches of Anna Howard Shaw," (Ph.D. dissertation). University of Wisconsin, 1960. Excerpt posted at http://gos.sbs.edu/s/shaw.html

Mackenzie, Midge. *Shoulder to Shoulder—A Documentary.* New York: Alfred A. Knopf, 1975.

Nelson, Barbara J., and Najma Chowdhury (editors). *Women and Politics Worldwide.* New Haven, Connecticut: Yale University Press, 1994.

"Parade Protest Arouses Senate." *The New York Times* (New York), March 5, 1913: 8.

Partnow, Elaine. *The New Quotable Woman.* New York: Facts On File, 1992.

Paul, Alice. *Alice Paul,* Regional Oral History Office, University of California, Berkeley. November 1972 and May 1973.

"Police Idly Watched Abuse of Women." *The New York Times* (New York, New York), March 7, 1913: 1.

Sherr, Lynn. *Failure Is Impossible—Susan B. Anthony in Her Own Words.* New York: Times Books, 1995.

_____ and Jurate Kazickas. *Susan B. Anthony Slept Here—A Guide to American Women's Landmarks.* New York: Times Books, 1976, 1994.

Sims, Anastatia. "Armageddon in Tennessee: The Final Battle Over the Nineteenth Amendment." *One Woman, One Vote—Rediscovering the Woman Suffrage Movement,* edited by Marjorie Spruill Wheeler, 332–52. Troutdale, Oregon: NewSage Press, 1995.

Spring, Joel. *The American School 1642–1985.* New York, New York: Longman, 1986.

Stansell, Christine. "The Seneca Falls Convention." *Days of Destiny—Crossroads in American History,* edited by James M. McPherson and Alan Brinkley, 132–43. New York: Dorling Kindersley, 2001.

Stanton, Elizabeth Cady, Susan B. Anthony, and Matilda Joslyn Gage (editors). *History of Woman Suffrage (Volume I).* Salem, New Hampshire: Ayer Company, 1985 (reprint).

Stevens, Doris. *Jailed for Freedom.* New York: Boni and Liveright, 1920.

On Maryland Day, suffragists from that state demonstrated their interest in voting rights during the opening weeks of White House picketing in 1917. The thoughts of a passing girl on rollerskates (center) might be miles away—or they might be focused on considering whether or not she would be permitted to vote when she grew up.

_____ and Carol O'Hare (editor). *Jailed for Freedom, American Women Win the Vote.* Troutdale, Oregon: NewSage Press, 1995.

Stiehm, Judith. *Nonviolent Power— Active and Passive Resistance in America.* Lexington, Massachusetts: D.C. Heath, 1972.

"Suffrage Invasion Is on in Earnest." *The New York Times* (New York), March 2, 1913: 15.

"Suffrage's Biggest Show." *The New York Times* (New York), March 9,1913: Inaugural section, part 3.

"Sylvester Shocked at Insults to Women." *The New York Times* (New York), March 9, 1913: 3.

Terborg-Penn, Rosalyn. "African American Women and the Woman Suffrage Movement." *One Woman, One Vote—Rediscovering the Woman Suffrage Movement,* edited by Marjorie Spruill Wheeler, 134–55. Troutdale, Oregon: NewSage Press, 1995.

_____ . *African American Women in the Struggle for the Vote, 1850–1920.* Bloomington: Indiana University Press, 1998.

Thurner, Manuela. "'Better Citizens Without the Ballot': American Anti-Suffrage Women and Their Rationale During the Progressive Era." *One Woman, One Vote—Rediscovering the Woman Suffrage Movement,* edited by Marjorie Spruill Wheeler, 203–20. Troutdale, Oregon: NewSage Press, 1995.

U.S. Senate Committee on the District of Columbia. *Women's Suffrage and the Police, Three Senate Documents.* New York: Arno Press and *The New York Times,* 1971.

Van Voris, Jacqueline. *Carrie Chapman Catt: A Public Life.* New York: The Feminist Press at the City University of New York, 1987.

Ward, Geoffrey C., and Ken Burns. *Not for Ourselves Alone— The Story of Elizabeth Cady Stanton and Susan B. Anthony.* New York: Alfred A. Knopf, 1999.

Wheeler, Marjorie Spruill. *New Women of the New South: The Leaders of the Woman Suffrage Movement in the Southern States.* New York: Oxford University Press, 1993.

"Wilson Takes Office To-Day as 28th President." *The New York Times* (New York), March 4, 1913: 1.

"Women Await Order to Fall in Line." *The New York Times* (New York), March 3, 1913: 7.

COVER: At least three generations lived with the issue of "how long must women wait for liberty?" during the fight for the right to vote. The battle was drawing to a close by March 4, 1919, when Ella C. Thompson (holding banner) joined Alice Paul and other members of the National Woman's Party at a New York City demonstration against President Woodrow Wilson.

HALF-TITLE PAGE: Songs provided a lighthearted way to promote the cause of voting rights for women. One popular adaptation suggested: "Yankee Doodle, keep it up. Our brothers must not flout us. Mind the music, keep the step. They will not vote without us."

TITLE PAGE: Women wage earners protested their lack of voting rights during a "Labor Day" demonstration at the White House on Sunday, February 18, 1917. Usually the pickets took Sundays off, but laborers marched on that day because it was their only day away from work.

PAGE 112: A 20th-century suffragist in Massachusetts "recruited" the elephant from a traveling circus to bear a supportive banner for her cause during the show's opening parade through her small town.

BACK COVER: Purple for justice, white for purity of purpose, and, most of all, gold for courage, this grandmotherly woman seems to be explaining to her attentive companion. These three colors were among the symbols that women carried with them to victory in the 72-year fight for a woman's right to vote.

ABOUT THE AUTHOR: *With Courage and Cloth* is Ann Bausum's third book for National Geographic. She was drawn to the story of the struggle for women's voting rights in part through the vibrant characters who took up the cause. "All of us benefit from their achievements," she notes. "We can draw inspiration from their bravery, their ingenuity, and their determination, too." Ann met strong women early in her life as a graduate of the Madeira School, an all-girls high school outside of Washington, D.C. She volunteered on Capitol Hill and learned the importance of participatory government, especially voting. She lives in Beloit, Wisconsin—the first state to ratify the 19th Amendment—with her husband and two sons. Visit her on her Web site: www.AnnBausum.com.

ILLUSTRATIONS CREDITS: Photographs provided courtesy of the historic National Woman's Party, headquartered at the Sewall-Belmont House and Museum, Washington, D.C. (NWP), the Library of Congress Prints and Photographs Division (LC), the Library of Congress Manuscript Division, National Woman's Party Collection (LC-MD) and the Smithsonian Institution, National Museum of American History, Behring Center, Political History Collection (SI) are listed by the noted abbreviations.

Front cover, Bettmann/CORBIS; p. 1, Bettmann/CORBIS; p. 2, NWP #P1274; p. 4, NWP; p. 6, NWP; p. 8, SI #88-1331; p. 10, LC-USZ62-70382; p. 12, LC-USZ62-77359; p. 14,

LC-USZ62 26724; p. 16, LC-USZ62-98405; p. 20 up, LC-USZ62-48965; p. 20 low, LC-B613-02; p. 23, The Schlesinger Library, Radcliffe Institute, Harvard University, photo by Sarony's, N.Y., A 143-3a-17; p. 24, Denver Public Library, Western History Collection, Z-8811; p. 26, LC-USZC4-6471; p. 28, courtesy of Coline Jenkins/Elizabeth Cady Stanton Trust; pp. 30-31, NWP #P2006; p. 32, LC-USZ62-50048; pp. 36-37, NWP #P2159; p. 38, LC-B2-4112-10; p. 41, LC-USZ62-53233; p. 42, NWP #P1091; p. 43, NWP #P1076; pp. 44-45, NWP #P1310; p. 46, NWP; p. 48, LC-B633-21; p. 50, NWP #P2192; pp. 52-53, LC-MD; p. 56, NWP #P0851; p. 57, NWP; p. 58, NWP #P1382; p. 59, NWP; p. 60, NWP; p. 62, LC-USZ62-89761; p. 65, NWP #P1392; p. 66, NWP; p. 68, LC-USZ62-7089; p. 70, LC-USZ62-134204; p. 72, NWP; pp. 74-75, NWP #P2486; p. 77, courtesy of the Tennessee State Library and Archives (Josephine Pearson papers, box 1, folder 13, copy neg. #1437); p. 80, LC-USZ62-14447; p. 82, LC-B2-4549-13; p. 84, LC-USZ62-34302, reprinted with permission of the Dallas Morning News; pp. 86-87, Jo Freeman (www.JoFreeman.com); p. 88, LC, Theodor Horydczak collection, LC-H824-T-S07-101; pp. 90-91, SI #78-17195; p. 92, reprinted courtesy Nebraska State Historical Society RG2669.PH:5; p. 93, NWP #P0143; p. 94, LC-USZ62-110995; p 95, NWP; p. 96, courtesy of Coline Jenkins/Elizabeth Cady Stanton Trust; p. 97, LC-USZ62-119343, p. 108, LC-MD; p. 112, SI #75059; back cover, LC-USZ62-134210.

PUBLISHED BY THE
NATIONAL GEOGRAPHIC SOCIETY
John M. Fahey, Jr., *President and
Chief Executive Officer*
Gilbert M. Grosvenor,
Chairman of the Board
Nina D. Hoffman, *Executive Vice President,
President of Books and Education Publishing Group*
Ericka Markman, *Senior Vice President,
President of Children's Books and Education
Publishing Group*

STAFF FOR THIS BOOK
Nancy Laties Feresten, *Vice President,
Editor-in-Chief of Children's Books*
Bea Jackson, *Art Director, Children's Books*
Jennifer Emmett, *Project Editor*
Ruth Thompson, *Production Designer*
Janet Dustin, *Illustrations Assistant*
Carl Mehler, *Director of Maps*
Suzanne Patrick Fonda, *Editor*
Susan Kehnemui Donnelly, *Editorial Assistant*
Judith Klein, *Copy Editor*
Connie D. Binder, *Indexer*
R. Gary Colbert, *Production Director*
Lewis R. Bassford, *Production Manager*
Vincent P. Ryan, *Manufacturing Manager*

One of the world's largest nonprofit
scientific and educational organizations,
the National Geographic Society was
founded in 1888 "for the increase and
diffusion of geographic knowledge."
Fulfilling this mission, the Society
educates and inspires millions every day
through its magazines, books, television
programs, videos, maps and atlases,
research grants, the National Geographic
Bee, teacher workshops, and innovative
classroom materials. The Society is
supported through membership dues,
charitable gifts, and income from the
sale of its educational products. This
support is vital to National Geographic's
mission to increase global understanding and promote conservation of our
planet through exploration, research,
and education.

For more information, please call
1-800-NGS LINE (647-5463)
or write to the following address:
NATIONAL GEOGRAPHIC SOCIETY
1145 17th Street N.W.
Washington, D.C. 20036-4688 U.S.A.
Visit the Society's Web site at
www.nationalgeographic.com.